Life
in the
Millennium

Mona Johnian

Life
in the
Millennium

BRIDGE PUBLISHING
S. Plainfield, NJ

Scriptural references are taken from the *King James Version*, the *Amplified Bible* and the *New King James Version*.

Life in the Millennium by Mona Johnian
ISBN 0-88270-705-1
Copyright© 1992 by Mona Johnian

Revised and reprinted 1994

Published by:
Bridge Publishing, Inc.
2500 Hamilton Blvd.
South Plainfield, NJ 07080

Printed in the United States of America.

Contents

LIFE IN THE MILLENNIUM COMPANION INDEX

Foreword

Life in the Millennium is tremendously instructive, intriguing, impressive and inspirational.

Normally, one must search the diversified writings of multiplied authors to glean a limited amount of facts about Christ's thousand-year reign upon earth.

Mona Johnian's efforts, in just one volume, bring to light hundreds of breathtaking facts that make a believer yearn for that glorious moment.

Jack Van Impe

1

The New World Order

Unlimited Potential

Imagine what life could be like if all of us used one hundred percent of the capacity of our brains, as opposed to the ten percent or so we presently use. The products, discoveries, and insights for greater living that would come from five billion people at full mental productivity are beyond our ability to contemplate. Unbelievable as it may seem, those who will be alive during the Millennium will experience one thousand years of just such unhindered growth and development. The range of creative expression that is coming in the future will exceed anything we have ever imagined.

The phrase, "eye has not seen" means we have not built it, nor yet discovered it through a microscope or telescope. "Ear has not heard" means that we have not composed it in words or music or any other sound vibration. "Neither has it entered into the heart of man the things which God has prepared for those who love Him," means that since the imagination of man has been largely wasted on "survival," it has never really been set free to discover the things that will truly benefit society. The "things God has prepared," however, does not mean that God has done everything for us in the future, so that we have only to retire into some kind of non-productive millennial fantasy. What God has prepared is a mind that is patterned after His, with unlimited creative ability. Didn't Paul say we shall know even as we are also known? (1 Corinthians 13:12) As God knows creation, creation will know Him—His thoughts, His ways of bringing life into every situation.

Once the mind is no longer limited by encroaching death, and its full potential is energized and released by the power of God, man will be able to live and produce at the divine level that was originally intended for us. God has prepared a realm of potential that will awaken strains within us we never knew existed. It will be the imagination Adam had before the curse of death began to rob him. We may now possess one, two, three talents, but in the Millennium we will blossom as cells of the body multiply in the presence of life-giving nutrition.

A mind separated from God is bound by the present limitations of the fallen world. Even the greatest minds have only a fraction of man's original intellectual capabilities. A genius in our day is no more than an infant when compared to the man of Eden, and the man of the future, after he has undergone 1,000 years of divinely stimulated thinking. More than two-thirds of all the scientific and technological knowledge we possess today was discovered in the past 500 years. Cave men would be shocked to wander into a twentieth-century space center. Even so, a scientist from today, if he could wander into a twenty-fifth century laboratory, would be overwhelmed. The things God has prepared for His millennial people are things that man does not, as yet, have the vocabulary to discuss. There are things man will discover, and enter into and help build, as naturally as we now launch a rocket. Space was never closed to man except in his limited imagination. The Millennium will remove these limitations.

God's commission to Adam was not that he should lie around in some kind of celluloid "Shangri-la" and be nothing. Adam was equipped and commissioned to be productive and to multiply in all of his divine capabilities. So it will be again in the future.

From time to time, reporters compile a documentary on the humanitarian efforts of medicine and they air these findings on television. "Missions of mercy" into third-world countries for life-changing medical procedures always grip the hearts of viewers. Huge growths, deformed faces, blind eyes, skin diseases are rampant in large parts of the world. One realistic look at afflictions in any nation tells us that we are a planet living under a curse. But by the grace of God, this is not a permanent situation. The legal rights to remove the curse have already been transacted through the sacrificial death of Jesus. By the law of the spirit realm, where curses originate, Jesus has challenged the source of the curse and won the court decision to restore man and his world to wholeness.

If it all sounds too far-fetched, then ask yourself this question: If there were not a "power" that has the capability of overcoming a curse, then what motivates doctors to reverse physical deformities? Why don't we just accept deformities as normal? What makes us want to change disfigured faces and bodies? Is it not obvious that something within us says, "This is not right, and it should be corrected!" That "something" is the Spirit of God who was sent to earth to witness to the fact of God and His intentions of good things for the human race.

The Millennium is a time coming on this earth when the curse of Satan is going to be lifted, and mankind is going to experience its finest hour. It will be actual years when the best of man will rise to the surface, and each person will begin to aim for his highest performance. Instead of the energies of man having to be spent on "corrective" endeavors, we will have time to pursue creative talents that will enhance a society that is breaking out on all fronts. We will be people with 20-20 vision who don't have to use our resources to make eyeglasses and perform eye surgery. Good health is normal. Sickness and disease are abnormal. Crime and destruction are the aliens. Sin is the robber. In the Millennium, men's minds are going to be free to see this truth, and the necessary corrections will follow. Righteous living, properly understood, tastes better than our favorite dessert. The spirit of Man has yet to indulge in heaven's finest cuisine!

The world system operates under a blanket of deception. Satan has yet to be physically evicted. His system, although legally defeated, has not yet been removed. His curse still operates wherever it can find people who do not know his tactics. Satan is illegal. But this does not stop him from operating as though he were a normal part of the human experience through people who give him license to practice. And since two thirds of the world still lives in spiritual blindness, Satan has ample opportunity to afflict millions.

The problem is spiritual. The cure is spiritual. The answer to the earth's dilemma lies in finding a "surgeon" who can not only cut away its deformities, but can also remove the source of its afflictions.

The Master Surgeon

According to Isaiah, God is that Master Surgeon. "For my sword shall be bathed in heaven," God declares. "And all the host of heavens shall be dissolved, and the heavens shall be rolled together as a scroll; and all their host shall fall down as the leaf falls from the vine, and as a falling fig from a fig tree." (Isaiah 34:4-5)

The truth of the future is this, at an appointed hour that only He knows, God is going to shake himself, arise from His celestial habitation, and sound a note that will penetrate His entire creation. Zechariah says God will sound the trumpet, He will put that sacred instrument to His omnipotent lips, and Gabriel will call with a loud voice. God will then take in hand His great knife and with one skillful slash, He is going to cut Satan's headquarters right out of the second heavens. God will bathe His sword in Satan's blood. In the twinkling of an eye, Satan and all his angelic hosts will come falling out of the sky as dried leaves fall to the ground in late autumn. As overripe figs, they will hit the earth with a pelting thud. And who will be here waiting to greet them? Jesus said, "I beheld Satan as lightning fall from heaven." Jesus will be waiting!

Positioned with His royal army, Jesus and His saints will observe a phenomenon never before seen by angel or mortal. God's day of surgery will be the spectacle of the ages. Like cancer cells of infection and confusion, Satan and his powers are going to come tumbling, screeching, ungracefully splattering all over the carnage of this war-torn battleground called earth, declaring the greatest act of surgery ever performed in heaven or on earth.

Satan, the one who has been behind the controversy over Israel; Satan, the one who for 6,000 years has deceived mankind into thinking we could come up with the answers to life; Satan, the one who has afflicted our bodies, destroyed our children, and built all our cemeteries; this same Satan and all his vast evil network will be slashed out the abdomen of heaven and confronted face to face with the Author who wrote Satan, sin and death out of the script before they ever applied for the starring roles.

Frame of Time

This book is designed to take the mysticism out of the Millennium, and we are going to discover that the millennium is actually a frame of time—"one thousand years"—roped off by God for a specific work. It is a period of time when God will prepare the earth and all creation to wed itself to heaven in a permanent relationship. Heaven and earth are destined for the marriage altar.

Marriage has fallen on hard times during the present generation. Satan is making every effort to blur the pattern of things to come. Jesus said divorce is unacceptable to God, except in the case of violation of the marriage vows. Marriage was originally designed to be permanently binding because it represents an eternal kingdom principle.

It has been a custom since ancient times for a bride to spend several months, even years, preparing herself for her wedding day. I once read of a tribe in Africa that requires the bride-to-be to lie in a tent every day for one year. During this time her feet are bathed in oil until all the crust is cleared away and her feet become as tender as a new-born baby.

For one thousand years God is going to bathe the earth in the oil of the Spirit and truth. Every crust of sin is going to be cleared away.

It is the time referred to by the Apostle Paul as, "the restoration of all things."

The old order of things is going to be done away with, and a new world order is coming in. There will be a new form of government, a new order of worship, and a new standard of moral behavior among men. It will be a divine order administered by the Son of God.

Messiah's New World Order

> For unto us a Child is born, unto us a Son is given; and the government will be upon His shoulder. And His name will be called Wonderful, Counselor, Mighty God, Everlasting Father, Prince of Peace. Of the increase of His government and peace there will be no end, upon the throne of David and over His kingdom, to order it and establish it with judgment and justice from that time forward, even forever. The zeal of the Lord of hosts will perform this. (Isaiah 9:6-7)

Messiah Yeshua–Jesus, the Anointed of God, will establish God's order of things on this earth, and man will learn to live according to the laws of life. Death and every ac-tion that leads to destruction are set to be outlawed during the period of millennial restoration. Nothing that harms or destroys will be allowed to continue.

His form of government and the results of Messiah's New World Order are described by Isaiah as the outworking of the mind of God.

The Spirit of the Lord shall rest upon Him, the Spirit of wisdom and understanding, the spirit of counsel and might, the Spirit of knowledge and of the fear of the Lord. His delight is in the fear of the Lord, and He shall not judge by the sight of His eyes, nor decide by the hearing of His ears; but with righteousness He shall judge the poor, and decide with equity for the meek of the earth; He shall strike the earth with the rod of His mouth, and with the breath of His lips He shall slay the wicked. Righteousness shall be the belt of His loins, and faithfulness the belt of His waist. The wolf also shall dwell with the lamb, the leopard shall lie down with the young goat, the calf and the young lion and the fatling together; and a little child shall lead them. The cow and the bear shall graze; their young ones shall lie down together; and the lion shall eat straw like the ox. The nursing child shall play by the cobra's hole, and the weaned child shall put his hand in the viper's den. (Isaiah 11:2-8)

God has a mind to destroy death and evil completely. By His Spirit and under the administration of His Son, His plan will be implemented for 1,000 years. It will be a time when nothing that harms or destroys will be allowed to continue. "They shall not hurt nor destroy in all My holy mountain, for the earth shall be full of the knowledge of the Lord as the waters cover the sea." (Isaiah 11:9)

Many Scriptures we live and draw strength from today will actually have their complete fulfillment in the Millennium. Hebrews 11 tells us that even God's first covenant with Abraham, for the land of Canaan, has yet to be fully realized.

There is hardly a believer who would say he has been able to fulfill his mission in life, and respond to every hunger of his heart to know and serve God. Somehow, we always fall short of full satisfaction. Sickness, financial setbacks, family problems—an ominous vulture always seems to be circling overhead, waiting to pick off a part of our otherwise victorious venture. And strange as it may seem, these are the results of living in a world ordered by perverted worship.

To initiate the complete cure for the problems of the world, from the moment Jesus sets His feet upon the Mount of Olives, first and foremost He will establish a new order of worship for Israel and all nations that want to be blessed during the Millennium.

> And it shall come to pass that everyone who is left of all the nations which came against Jerusalem shall go up from year to year to worship the King, the Lord of hosts, and to keep the Feast of Tabernacles. And it shall be that which ever of the families of the earth do not come up to Jerusalem to worship the King, the Lord of hosts, on them there will be no rain...In that day "HOLINESS TO THE LORD" shall be engraved on the bells of the horses. The pots in the Lord's house shall be like the bowls before the altar. Yes, every pot in Jerusalem and Judah shall be holiness to the Lord of hosts. Everyone who sacrifices shall come and take them and cook in them. In that day there shall be no longer a Canaanite in the house of the Lord of hosts. (Zechariah 14: 16-17,20-21)

This new order of worship will be the key that will set the minds of men free to become all God originally intended when He created man. It will not be an instantaneous maturity, although Israel will be converted in a day. But spiritual conversion from darkness to light, from error to truth, will develop wisely, effectively and supernaturally. Through the strategy of qualified leader-ship, God will appoint His people to govern, teach righteousness, restrain unsound behavior, and reorganize the worship system of the entire human race.

A New Worship Order

Today we often hear the proposal of a "New World Order." But there can be no new world order until there is a new "Worship" order—worship in Spirit and in truth. The worship of man will die at Armageddon. The true worship of God will then commence, and with true worship will come the release of man's finest hour.

According to the prophets, this worship will find its fountainhead in Jerusalem. When Zechariah declared that, "there shall be no longer a Canaanite in the house of the Lord," he exposed the utter cleansing that is coming in worship. The "Canaanite" is a term that goes back to the days of Noah.

After the Flood, Noah planted a vineyard. At the end of the harvest season, he drank to the point of intoxication. He had made the wine from his harvest. The Bible is not clear about all the events that took place while Noah lay in his tent in a drunken state. It says only that he was uncovered and his son Ham came into the tent and saw the nakedness of his father (See Genesis 9:21-22).

Whatever occurred in this situation was greatly displeasing to God. It was unholy. As a result, God spoke a permanent curse on one of Ham's sons named Canaan. For this reason the Canaanites came to be looked upon as the people of the lowest possible position, "a servant of servants." Jesus put them in the spiritual category of dogs–

undeserving of the Father's blessings, uncircumcised, without covenant, unsaved.

With an Eye on God

Zechariah said that during the Millennium there will be no doubting, no compromises, no immorality, no unsaved Canaanites worshiping in Jerusalem. Only God-fearing reverence will take place in the presence of Messiah. Out of His sanctuary will go the pattern for worship in spirit and in truth for all the world.

After 6,000 years of sin in the world and compromise in the Church, the true pattern of worship has been severely altered. The word "worship" cannot be defined by the single act of going to church. Worship is an all-encompassing way of life. By definition, it describes a life that is lived with an eye on God.

Imagine what drastic changes would occur in society if every person lived with "an eye on God." I mean the God of the Bible.

In today's society, "family" has been redefined as any number of people living under the same roof. But if we define the word in the moral sense with "an eye on God," we will find it means a man and a woman committed in the legal bonds of marriage.

Also in today's society, "morality" has been redefined to cover any arrangement that people find comfortable for them personally. But if we define the word with "an eye on God" we will find it means sex between a man and a woman in the bonds of marriage, period.

Business ethics, honesty in government, justice for the innocent—imagine what society will be when every person makes his or her decisions with an eye on God.

A brilliant young man came to me with this proposition: "What should I do? My boss at work is good to me. I have come up with an invention that has great possibility. I have invited other godly men to come into partnership with me in this venture, and they agreed. When my boss heard of my venture he called me in and demanded a sizable portion of this venture which would eliminate my other partners."

What should this young entrepreneur do? The answer is clear—he must make his decision as though he were standing in the presence of God, with an eye on Him. Why? Because he is a worshiper of God. And making decisions that measure up to God's standards is the only way to worship in spiritual truth and to reap God's rewards.

Eusebeia means a life lived with an eye on God. *Asebeai* means just the opposite where both eyes are turned in on self, where self becomes the object of worship and the motive behind every action. This is why true worship will be the first thing Messiah will restore during His millennial reign.

The Loss of Spiritual Vision

With the Adamic loss of brain power came the loss of most of our spiritual senses. The ability to recognize and respect "sacred" things has all but disappeared. Doctors work hard to combat the loss of natural hearing and sight. During the Millennium, God is going to send out spiritual technicians who will help to restore the full range of hearing contained in the spirit of man. It will be an auditory ability that will enable man to learn things about life that will be absolutely amazing. There are angel songs and conversation going on all about us now that would thrill and enlighten us beyond measure if only we could open our eyes and ears to hear sounds on that supernatural level.

During the closing days of human history, spiritual sight and hearing will almost totally disappear. Most of the world will not be able to see or hear God at all. Most do not see or hear Him now.

Alexander Solzenitsyn said, "If I were called to identify briefly the principle trait of the entire twentieth century, hereto I would be unable to find anything more precise...than to repeat once again, men have forgotten God."

The Millennium is coming to help men see and hear and remember. The servants of sin and the Canaanite level of living will no longer hold key positions in society. Such people will be replaced by those whose minds have been renewed through a lifestyle of true worship—people whose intelligence quotient will tap into that 85% of unused brain power we haven't used since Eden.

What we want to do is understand more about how God is going to fulfill this thousand years of clean-up and revitalization of our war-torn planet. What will the earth be like with Satan restrained from directly influencing the hearts and minds of men? Have you ever wondered? Will all men turn immediately to God? Will pollution disappear? Will we have need of worship services? What will happen to the various nations? Who will rule them? Let us turn now to the Bible and see what God has to say about this period of time, beginning with the events that lead into the 1,000 years of restoration.

2

The Twilight of the Tribulation Passover

Almost 4,000 years ago, a feeble patriarch leaned on his staff while he spoke the word of God over his 12 sons. When he came to his fourth son, speaking above and beyond time, Jacob said to him:

> Judah, you are he whom your brothers shall praise; your hand shall be on the neck of your enemies; your father's children shall bow down before you. Judah is a lion's whelp [cub]; from the prey, my son, you have gone up. He bows down, he lies down as a lion; and as a lion, who shall rouse him? The scepter shall not depart from Judah, nor a lawgiver from between his feet, until Shiloh comes; and to Him shall be the obedience of the people. Binding his donkey to the vine, and his donkey's colt to the choice vine, he washed his garments in wine, and his clothes in the blood of grapes. His eyes are darker than wine, and his teeth whiter than milk. (Genesis 49:8-12)

Approximately 250 years after this word was spoken, the descendants of Jacob [Israel] left Egypt. Free from slavery, they were on their way back home to Canaan. Coming to the land of Moab, this massive company of people pitched their tents on the plains, on the other side of the Jordan River near Jericho.

The king of Moab, a descendant of Lot, was threatened by this million or more people camping in his country, and he called for a prophet to come and curse Jacob's descendants, Israel. When the prophet came, this is what he delivered from the Lord:

> How lovely are your tents, O Jacob! Your dwellings, O Israel! Like valleys that stretch out, like gardens by the riverside, like aloes planted by the Lord, like cedars beside the waters. He shall pour water from his buckets, and his seed shall be in many waters. His king shall be higher than Agag, and his kingdom shall be exalted. God brings him out of Egypt; he has strength like a wild ox; he shall consume the nations, his enemies; he shall break their bones and pierce them with his arrows. He bows down, he lies down as a lion; and as a lion, who will rouse him?' Blessed is he who blesses you, and cursed is he who curses you. (Numbers 24:5-9)

Strikingly similar, here we have two of the most powerful words ever given to man by God. Clothed in symbolism, they are nonetheless an explanation of God's clear intention concerning the culmination of human history and the millennial reign of Christ on the earth. Surely Judah did not understand the full extent of what his father had spoken over him, nor did the king of Moab understand when it was repeated some 250 years later. It would take

2,000 years more, and many prophets, to fully clarify God's intentions. But little by little the plan has unfolded, and today we can see the picture almost completed.

As slaves in Egypt, it took the plague of death to set Israel free to go home to the land God gave their father Abraham. Judah was among them. It was the first great Passover—when the blood of the lamb was applied to their door posts, that the "death angel" might pass over the house of Israel. But it would not be the last time their lives would be spared. For Judah has yet to prevail over his enemies. There is coming a day when the wrath of God will visit the earth one last time, and when Judah emerges from this day, the Passover will be a perpetual mark upon them forever. Shiloh is coming. "Judah, you are he whom your brothers shall praise."

Bound to a Land

When a person has hold of something that will destroy him if he lets go, that person cannot afford to turn loose. The axiom is, "He's got a tiger by the tail."

The land of Israel is a tiger. The nation Israel has a divine assignment to hold on. If they let go, they're dead. Yet, the world keeps asking how much longer they can last. The nations of the earth have been scratching their heads for 4,000 years. Why are the Jews so stubborn? How much is a piece of real estate worth? Why not give up that tiny piece of Mediterranean property and get the United Nations to give them some land where they can live in peace? Naturally speaking, it would make sense. It's dry; it's parched; it has to be irrigated, and it has a history of war 6,000 years long. No land is worth the sacrifice it takes for Israel to remain surrounded by hostile governments.

Stubborn Jews? Not exactly. Even if they wanted, the Jews can never turn loose the land of Israel. They are locked in by the mandate of God, who never alters what has gone out of His mouth. When God said, "The scepter shall not depart from Judah, nor a lawgiver from between his feet, until Shiloh comes," He commissioned the Jews to hold on to Israel until Shiloh—the Messiah—arrives to set up His government.

It was not enough that Judah hold on to Israel until Messiah was born in Bethlehem. They must maintain the land until He comes again, to establish His eternal kingdom on the throne of David. "And the Lord God shall give unto him the throne of his father David" (Luke 1:32).

The government of heaven has its earthly headquarters sited for the land of Israel. God has a covenant with that land. The Jews have been given the responsibility of maintaining that headquarters until the Governor arrives, even though they have a history of losing it to invading powers.

Clearly, Israel has never fully understood the spiritual claim of this land on their nation. Because of their own spiritual rebellions, their history is marked by wars, losses, and the regaining of their responsibility. But God has never budged one inch. Even when Israel was driven out by the Romans in A.D.70, God put a hook in their nose and drove them back to Canaan in 1948. It took great pain and devastation, but Israel went back to their assignment. Israel has always been small in number, compared to the world population. Yet the natural working out of the destiny of the human race was laid upon their shoulders.

> • To the Jews was given the task of being first to walk in covenant with Jehovah God.

- To the Jews was given the task of maintaining the land of His covenant.

- To them was given the task of maintaining the laws of God.

- To them was given the task of maintaining the message and hope of the Deliverer—Messiah.

- To the Jew was given the task of giving birth to the Messiah.

- To them was given the task of receiving the New Covenant.

- To them was given the task of being first to spread the "gospel" of God's New Covenant with both the Jews and the Gentiles.

No wonder Jacob prophesied of him, "Judah is a lion's cub! With the prey, my son, you have gone high up [the mountain]; he stooped down, he crouched as a lion, and as a lioness; who dares provoke and rouse him?" (Genesis 49:10, Amplified).

It was the tribe of Judah, fourth son of Jacob, who gave birth to the Messiah. There shall come forth a Rod from the stem of Jesse, and a Branch shall grow out of his roots. ...He raised up for them David as king, to whom also He gave testimony and said, 'I have found David, the son of Jesse, a man after My own heart, who will do all My will.' From this man's seed, according to the promise, God raised up for Israel a Savior—Jesus. (Isaiah 11:1; Acts 13:22,23)

19

Judah was the ancestor of Jesse; Jesse was the father of David; David was the father of Solomon and Nathan. Joseph came from the line of Solomon; Mary from the line of Nathan. Jesus was born of Mary in the house of Joseph. And it was all the responsibility of the Jews to let it be lived out in them. Is it any wonder that the Jews sit crouched like a lion ready for attack? Every time they turn loose, God goes after them and drags them back to their divine mandate. "Until Shiloh—Messiah—comes—Judah, you are to occupy! You may have to pay with your blood, Israel— but occupy!"

And the Jews occupy. Many of them do it blindly, but that "something within" continues to draw them irresistibly to their task.

The *Aliya* (return of Jews to Israel) is alive and strong. They are preparing the world for the Millennium. But the Millennium—as was the exodus from Egypt—is going to be preceded by dramatic resistance. The Pharaoh (Satan) of this generation is just as determined to prevent God's covenant from being ratified as the Pharaoh that Moses encountered 3,500 years ago.

The principalities and powers in the heavenlies are aligning themselves for the battle of the ages. The stage for the world theater is the Middle East. Anyone who forgets this is not viewing the world as it is in real terms, but as it appears in the natural realm.

People, including the Church, have misunderstood the plan of redemption for the simple reason they view events with a natural eye. Majoring on the personality of the Jewish nation—instead of their divine mandate, has caused us to view redemption—salvation—as having been finished at the death and resurrection of Jesus.

The price for redemption was completed and paid in full at Calvary. But the complete plan of redemption will not occur until Jesus returns.

Peter said of Jesus that He is the one "Whom the heaven must receive until the times of restitution [complete restoration] of all things, which God hath spoken by the mouth of his holy prophets since the world began" (Acts 3:21).

Every time we take Holy Communion, the Eucharist, Paul said we are proclaiming Christ's death "until He comes." This period of history is the "until age." Both the nation of Israel and the Church are in the land of Goshen. We are exactly where Israel was in Egypt. We have lived well.

The Church has risen to great liturgical, architectural and cultural heights. We have experienced the respect and tolerance of Egypt. But the time is soon coming when we will be despised, feared and persecuted because of our unmistakable mandate.

The Church has yet to demonstrate the resurrection power of a people delivered from Egypt. When Israel first went into Egypt, Joseph, son of Jacob, was second in command of that great empire. But a Pharaoh came into office who didn't know Joseph, and respect for Israel quickly turned to disrespect and persecution. And just before the great day of Passover deliverance, Israel experienced its darkest hour.

Earth's brightest hour will be the Millennium. Its darkest hour will be the days immediately preceding the millennial dawn. Darkness precedes the dawn but it does not prevent it.

Israel is climbing the mountain now with the prey in its mouth, as Jacob foretold. "Judah is a lion's cub! With the prey, my son, you have gone high up [the mountain]" (Genesis 49:10).

Israel is not the Lion, but they are the cub with the prey between its teeth.

"Natural" Israel is holding on to the land. "Adopted" Israel—the Church—is holding on to the promise and spreading the gospel. "And if ye [the Church] be Christ's, then are ye Abraham's seed, and heirs according to the promise" (Galatians 3:29).

Both the Church and Israel have a mandate to occupy until the Lord comes. Both must be taken into account if we will understand the Scriptures concerning end-time events accurately.

The Deliverer will come. Pharaoh will be notified. His greatest resistance will soon become obvious. We are rapidly approaching the twilight of the "tribulation" passover, and the greatest upheavals the world has ever seen, as well as the greatest demonstrations of the power of God.

First comes twilight; then comes midnight; then comes the dawn!

3

The Coming Exodus

In one of his letters to the Church, the Apostle Paul makes a startling statement regarding the exodus of Israel from bondage in Egypt. Beginning with the cloud of God that overshadowed Israel to their crossing the Jordan, Paul concludes all their trials and triumphs by saying, "Now all these things happened to them as examples..." (1 Corinthians 10:11).

Examples?

Right off, we stop and ask ourselves, "Examples of what and for whom?" One does not give an example of something unless he expects that situation to be repeated. If Israel's exodus from Egypt was an example, then obviously another "Exodus" is going to occur which will be similar in principle.

Let us go back now and read Paul's entire statement on this startling possibility, and see if we can learn what he means. Speaking of the exodus, Paul writes, "Now all these things happened to them as examples, and they were written for our admonition, on whom the ends of the ages have come" (1 Corinthians 10:11).

What happened to Israel just prior to and during the exodus, approximately 3,500 years ago, is being repeated in the last generations. So important and vital were the first set of exodus events that God had Moses record them for our admonition [warning], upon whom the ends of the world are come.

Moreover, the second great sermon that followed the outpouring of the Holy Spirit, delivered by the Apostle Peter, was also about this very subject. In speaking to those Jewish people who had not believed in Jesus before His crucifixion, Peter said,

> Repent therefore and be converted, that your sins may be blotted out, so that times of refreshing may come from the presence of the Lord, and that He may send Jesus Christ, who was preached to you before, whom heaven must receive until the times of restoration of all things, which God has spoken by the mouth of all His holy prophets since the world began. For Moses truly said to the fathers, 'The Lord your God will raise up for you a Prophet like me from your brethren. Him you shall hear in all things, whatever He says to you. (Acts 3:19-22)

All the prophets foretold the coming of a great Deliverer—like Moses—who would be from the nation Israel. This Prophet would not only deliver His nation, but everything in creation. God's people of Israel, believing Gentiles, even the earth itself would be fully and finally delivered from the curse of sin and death by this Prophet who is presently being retained in heaven until the appointed time of the final restoration.

Did you know that since 3,600 B.C., the world has known only 292 years of peace? Since then, there have been 14,532 wars in which 3,640,000,000 people have been killed. Someone has suggested that the value of the destruction of these wars would pay for a golden belt around the world 91.2 miles in width and about 33 feet thick. This translated into human services would bring this world very close to paradise.

The Millennium is coming. The earth is destined for a time of refreshing [Greek: fresh air] in the presence of the Lord. We are bound for the promised land. But as Israel experienced when they faced Canaan, I believe the 1,000 years of Christ's rule on the earth will be a time of increasing restoration. I do not believe restoration will happen overnight at the Second Coming of Christ. The overwhelming weight of evidence supports a work of moral purification and spiritual training of the nations, taming of the animals, healing of the air, land and waters that will occur over a period of time.

The Bible has devoted considerable space to discussing the changes we can expect during the period of 1,000 years when Jesus will be ruling from Jerusalem. There will be environmental clean up, dramatic shifts in government policies, utter collapse of all immoral institutions, and a total restructuring of the role of worship in society. Some institutions will undergo purification and remain, some will pass into oblivion. But before we get into all the wonderful possibilities of a society based on justice, instead of selfishness and greed, let us go back to the original pattern of the first exodus, and find out how it is all going to unfold.

The Birth of the First Church

A famine in the land of Canaan (modern-day Israel), drove Jacob, the grandson of Abraham, down into Egypt in search of food. At first the Israelites were well received, and co-existed successfully with the Egyptians, even though the Egyptian culture was pagan. The Bible says ". . .The children of Israel were fruitful and increased abundantly, multiplied and grew exceedingly mighty; and the land was filled with them" (Exodus 1:7).

But it was a situation destined to be drastically altered. There is no such thing as a permanent, peaceful coexistence between the Church and the world. Anytime the Church and the world seek to become permanent co-inhabitants of this planet, God does two things: He reminds His people that they are called out of the world system, and He judges the world for its sin and rebellion. Israel was the first Church. When God sent His call to Israel to come out of Egypt, He issued His first commission to establish a Church. Israel in the wilderness represents the initial birth of a called-out people. The Apostle Paul called Israel "the church in the wilderness" (Acts 7:38). The word church, *ekklesia*, means simply "called out ones." Israel was the first nation to be called out to worship the true and living God. It was with them that God established His first covenant on a national scale.

Listen to the word God sent to Pharaoh, regarding His intentions: ". . .Let My people go, that they may hold a feast to Me in the wilderness" (Exodus 5:1). A people called out to worship God is the purpose of the Church. Everything else we do and say points toward that one purpose—that we may worship God and bring others to know and worship Him.

Years ago, the church fathers seeking, to summarize the whole duty of man, established this one truth; "The chief end of man is to glorify God." The calling out of Israel, and the subsequent covenant God made with them in the wilderness, was the beginning of the Church, as well as the beginning of the end of the system of sin on the earth.

Fifteen hundred years following the first exodus, the "former rains" fell from heaven at the Feast of Weeks—or Pentecost—in Jerusalem and a New Covenant was established with God's Old Testament Church. It was time for the salvation of the Gentiles as well as the Jews, and the Church as we know it today was born.

There is coming one more "calling out" named the "latter rain" when God will again re-enact the Passover and the Exodus, for the greatest harvest of souls and the greatest judgment of sin the world has ever seen.

Former and Latter Rains

For a moment let us take a brief look at the terms "former and latter rains," as they tell us something about the way God has scheduled His great end-time harvest. As Israel was leaving Egypt and heading for Canaan, God made a covenant wherein He promised:

> And it shall be that if you diligently obey My commandments which I command you today, to love the Lord your God and serve Him with all your heart and with all your soul, then I will give you the rain for your land in it season, the early rain and the latter rain, that you may gather in your grain, your new wine, and your oil. (Deuteronomy 11:13-14)

The "former rain" was the early rain that fell in October to moisten the parched soil and prepare it for sowing. This represents the outpouring of the Holy Spirit on dry, parched Israel fifteen hundred years after they had come out of Egypt and strayed away from God. The "latter rain" was the rain that fell in March to bring the crops to maturity—and it represents the outpouring of the Spirit yet to come for the final kingdom harvest.

For confirmation of this let us turn to the words of the prophet Joel: "Be glad then, ye children of Zion, and rejoice in the Lord your God: for he hath given you the former rain moderately, and he will cause to come down for you the rain, the former rain, and the latter rain in the first month" (Joel 2:23).

When Israel went out of Egypt, the "former rain" fell moderately. At Pentecost it fell more abundantly. But this gentle rain of the Holy Spirit was nothing compared to what God is going to do when He sends the "Latter Rain" on the earth for the great millennial harvest. Just as He moved in Egypt, as Israel prepared herself to exodus, God is going to pull His giant fingers as a fine-tooth comb across this earth, from one end to the other. By the time He is finished, all tangles will have been removed, sin will have been thoroughly judged, and righteousness thoroughly rewarded.

I believe the Millennium will be 1,000 years of restoration, when the knowledge of the Lord is going to be taught, unhindered, over every square inch of the earth's surface. There will be no government restrictions, no antagonistic officials, no pagan religious authorities threatening God's ministers. God's people will be assigned key positions in government, so that the knowledge of God will be allowed to cover this earth as naturally as waters cover the sea floor.

There will be no magic, automatic coverage of the earth with the knowledge of God; it will be taught. But just as the word spread about the God of Israel as they came out of Egypt, so the word will spread about the purified nation of Israel and the Church of Jesus Christ, as they begin their simultaneous commissions under the reign of the Messiah. Israel will be the lead nation on earth; the Church will be leaders in kingdom assignment.

Let us return to the first pattern for a closer look at just how things are going to develop, as we enter the day of the exodus.

The First Passover

Israel had grown comfortable in Egypt. They were prosperous, they were prestigious. They had earned their place in society, and they didn't have any plans for disrupting their comfortable position. But as we stated earlier, God is never going to allow His people to settle in with the world.

The Church keeps trying to prove itself a viable part of the world system. We keep hoping to gain recognition as a necessary institution. But if it is anything near to what it should be, the Church is a contradiction to the world's ideologies. It is a source of irritation, a challenge, and a badgering enemy.

I listened to a debate between two Catholic priests, regarding exorcism. "Exorcism is a doctrine of the faith and a ministry to suffering people," one priest maintained. But the contention of the other priest stemmed from his fear that "exorcism makes the Church look ridiculous in the eyes of the world."

The most ridiculous thing the Church can do is to try to appeal to the pride of human intellect—which is wholly incapable of appreciating even one spiritual thing. The world has the greatest respect for the Church that is doing the least "spiritual works." Humanitarian efforts they can understand to some extent. Holy Spirit works, such as casting out the emissaries of Satan—never! This is the reason God will not allow the Church and the world to become friends. Every time the Church settles into a comfortable co-existence with the world, God sends another reformation, another revival, and the feud starts all over again.

Israel was comfortable down in Egypt, but God had no intention of letting the two nations remain bosom buddies. Whereas Israel had once enjoyed special favor with the government, a Pharaoh eventually came to power who despised the Hebrews and used them as slave labor to build his magnificent cities.

Example #1:

There is coming a definite, irreparable separation between the Church and the world. Officially, legally, publicly, the world is going to turn against the people of God and seek to discredit them in the eyes of public opinion. Pharaoh raised up *Sarey Missim*—chiefs in government, men of rank, superintendents of public works—and put them over the Israelites, " to afflict them..." (Exodus 1:11). The word Moses used here for "afflict" is a term still in use today. It means to browbeat. Men of rank were given positions of leadership in order to browbeat the Israelites. It is a very effective method for silencing the opposition.

Anyone with a measure of spiritual understanding can see that browbeating is precisely the strategy still being used against believers in the world today. In America, for example, a once-popular church, prayer, and religious education have been totally eliminated from public schools and public functions. The Bible is no longer the standard of reference for social behavior, and the book itself is declared illegal in the classroom. All of this took place in one generation.

What a rude awakening Israel must have experienced when they suddenly found themselves being browbeaten and discredited among the very people who had once honored them. Isolated, excluded socially, professionally and ultimately financially, Israel quickly found themselves confined to the land of Goshen, with a new status in society. They were one of "those" people.

Moses records that, "...the Egyptians made the children of Israel to serve with rigor" (Exodus 1:13). The word rigor (Hebrew: perek) means to break apart. The taskmasters—men of rank—tried to break down the people, kill their unity, destroy their divine purpose, reduce them to servants of the world instead of servants of God.

In spite of the persecution, however, Moses said, "...the more they afflicted them, the more they multiplied and grew" (Exodus 1:12). God even gave the Hebrew women favor with the Egyptian midwives, and as a result the midwives helped the Hebrew children escape Pharaoh's death penalty.

Example #2:

God makes a distinction between His people and the world. In the midst of persecution, God's people can still expect to find the necessary favor and provision for overcoming their taskmasters. The Word says, "Where sin abounds grace does much more abound." The stronger the persecution, the greater the favor with God, and the more miraculous His provision.

Satan is as a "lion seeking whom he may devour," but he is confined to God's game reserve. There is never going to be a time when Satan will be turned loose to do "everything" he desires. God holds him to the rules of war. This means that those people who stay close to God will abide under His shadow of protection, regardless of the violence around them. Once Moses arrived on the scene to deliver Israel, and the plagues began to fall on Egypt, the land of Goshen did not suffer God's judgments. It is important to remember that God's people will not suffer His wrath on the world for its sins. God never punishes the innocent for the sins of the guilty. Guilty men often cause the innocent to suffer, but God never personally inflicts punishment on those who are faithful to Him.

We see this confirmed in God's sixth demand for Pharaoh to let His people go:

> And the Lord said to Moses, "Rise early in the morning and stand before Pharaoh as he comes out to the water. Then say to him, 'Thus says the Lord: "Let My people go, that they may serve Me. Or else, if you will not let My people go, behold, I will send swarms of flies on you and your servants, on your people and into your houses. The houses of the Egyptians shall be full of swarms of flies, and also the ground on which they stand. And in that day I will set apart the land of Goshen, in which My people dwell, that no swarms of flies shall be there, in order that you may know that I am the Lord in the midst of the land. I will make difference between My people and your people. Tomorrow this sign shall be." (Exodus 8:20-23)

This difference is again confirmed by the mouth of Jesus as He addresses the subject of the last generation for whom Moses recorded all His examples. Let us read His warning:

> But take heed to yourselves, lest your hearts be weighed down with carousing, drunkenness, and cares of this life, and that Day come on you unexpectedly. For it will come as a snare on all those who dwell on the face of the whole earth. (Luke 21:34-35)

What a word of encouragement! To those who understand the end-times, nothing that happens will shake or disturb them. The last days will not come unexpectedly on the informed people.

Example #3:

There will definitely be a company of overcomers who will survive and experience the great coming exodus. This fact alone is one of the most encouraging examples we can find among the events of the first exodus. Yes, Israel was afflicted in Egypt, but in spite of their persecution, a great company survived to enjoy the exodus!

Once the judgements begin to fall on the last generation—including the period of tribulation and the "Day of the Lord," the book of Revelation tells us that it will all occur within a seven-year frame of time. Daniel, John, and Jesus confirm the fact that the generation that sees the beginning of the plagues will also see the ending. Jesus said:

> . . .Look at the fig tree, and all the trees. When they are already budding, you see and know for yourselves that summer is now near. So you, likewise, when you see these things happening, know that the

> kingdom of God is near. Assuredly, I say to you, this generation will by no means pass away till all things are fulfilled. (Luke 21:29-32)

This tells us that the terrible judgments coming on the earth are limited. According to both Daniel and John, those days will not exceed seven years. Some theologians speculate that it is quite possible that Moses' contest with Pharaoh lasted no more than fifty days of intense conflict. Israel's bondage had been for more than 250 years.

Their journey in Egypt had lasted approximately 400 years. They had been away from their promised land a long, long time. But their most severe hardship was limited by the hand of God, as it has been limited in the tribulation of the last days.

> For then there will be great tribulation, such as has not been since the beginning of the world until this time, no, nor ever shall be. And unless those days were shortened, no flesh would be saved; but for the elect's sake those days will be shortened. (Matthew 24:21-22)

Sin has a long history on the earth—at least 6,000 years. But chaos has a short itinerary. It will be brief, thorough and totally under the control of God. For the world, it will spell the end; for the earth, it will spell healing; for the Church and Israel, it will spell purification and the beginning of eternity.

At our house we often play a game that goes like this: If you could experience any moment in history, which would it be? It's exciting to think of all the great events that have transpired on this earth for the past 6,000 years. To have heard the first raindrop inside that creaking old ark with Noah, would have been a hair-raising moment to remember. To have seen Elijah taken into heaven by a chariot of fire, accompanied by a host of angels, would have been life-changing encounter with power. To have trudged along with a simple company of Nazarenes on their way to register for the great Caesar, with the Son of God about to make His entrance into the world, would have been a moment in beauty unlike any other the soul could ever hope to experience. An unidentifiable stirring must have enveloped the hearts of Mary and Joseph as Bethlehem loomed on the horizon. But of all the events I could have witnessed, I always maintain that I would want to be among those sun-parched Israelites, who had waited all those years for deliverance, heard the message preached a thousand times, endured, hoped and dreamed of Canaan, only to find one morning that the day of redemption had finally arrived!

I believe I desire this experience above all others, because this is the day that is still in the future, for the Church as well as the nation Israel. The Deliverer is coming. With Him we will eat the Passover, and with Him we will restore the earth to a land flowing with milk and honey.

4

The Great Contest

The exodus experience is a contest. What happened in Egypt 3,500 years ago was a battle between the two greatest powers of the universe, being played out on the stage of Pharaoh's court. Represented by Moses and Pharaoh, it was actually God and Satan standing face to face, challenging one another for supremacy. The real opponents of this contest were neither strengthened nor diminished by their mortal representatives.

The courage of both Moses and Pharaoh, however, would make all the difference in how many people would experience the Passover and how many would fall victim to the death angel. The contest between God and Satan is never to prove one superior to the other. It is understood from the outset that the Creator is superior to the created.

The struggle that continually rages in the heavenlies is played out on earth for the sake of men. The contest is an effort to strengthen—not God—but God's hand in the earth, His wise and eternal standard. This is why faithful men are God's number-one priority. Faithfulness is foundational to establishing God's works. God said, "My servant Moses is...faithful in all mine house" (Numbers 12:7).

In writing of the last Gentile powers to rule the earth, John said, "These have one mind, and shall give their power and strength unto the beast (Antichrist). These shall make war with the Lamb, and the Lamb shall overcome them: for he is Lord of lords and King of kings: and they that are with him are called, and chosen, and faithful" (Revelation 17:13,14).

People who experience the coming exodus will be "called, and chosen, and faithful." Jesus said, "Many are called but few are chosen." Moses called the entire nation of Israel to make a three-week journey with him from Egypt to the land of Canaan, from bondage to liberty. But only the faithful actually went in to possess the promised land. Because of doubt and unbelief, Israel was made to wander forty years in the desert, during which time the unfaithful men and women died. Only the faithful were allowed to cross the Jordan and actually possess their full inheritance.

In a documentary I watched about the development of the human mind, medical scientists have discovered an amazing faculty in the brain called commitment. For example, when a child is born it is capable of learning any language. One language is no more difficult than the other.

However, once a mind commits to one specific language it shuts down to the sounds of other languages. Once it commits to know its mother, she becomes priority over other women and so forth. This is the way the scientists explained it: "Commitment to one set of knowledge blocks out other knowledge. However, through commitment comes two rewards: efficiency and stability." In other words, it is natural to commit. Commitment is normal and necessary to the human mind, in order to do its best.

What a revolutionary concept! This tells us that today's non-committal philosophy is unnatural and actually promotes inefficiency and instability. Relationships that demand no commitment are not as efficient as those that require it. It also tells us that people who want to change from one way of being to another, from one set of knowledge to another, must first make a commitment. Is this not what Jesus meant when He said, "You cannot serve two masters." From the banks of the Jordan we hear the ancient cry, "Choose you this day whom you will serve!"

Commitment, which is a twin partner of faithfulness, produces people who will experience the coming Passover and the great exodus the world has been waiting to witness.

Passover in the Sacraments

When Jesus was on earth, He left two sacraments to be observed by His followers until His return. These two sacraments were water baptism and the Lord's Supper (The Eucharist), and both these sacraments point to one event —the Passover—the shed blood of the lamb. Both sacraments remind us that without the shedding of blood there is no remission of sin. And both tell us that because of the "shedding of blood," death will pass over all who have the blood applied to their lives.

It was no coincidence that the last meal Jesus ate on earth before His death, was the Passover. Jesus was the Passover Lamb for Israel in Egypt; and He will be the Passover Lamb for the Church and Israel when the end-time Pharaoh (Antichrist) stands up and challenges God for His people once again.

Every time we take the Lord's Supper we are remembering not only what Jesus did, but what He is yet to do when He comes again. The Passover Lamb has been slain. The blood is now being applied to the lives of all believers. Judgment is soon to fall and the trumpet call will summon the Church to begin its exodus.

Let us now take a look at the "first pattern—exodus," as it occurred between Moses and Pharaoh, bearing in mind that these events are examples for the last generation and are written for our warning. (See 1 Corinthians 10:11.)

In the last chapter we listed three examples from Egypt that apply to the last generation. Let us now go to example four from our pattern and see what we find.

Example #4:

God first sends His Word before He sends judgment. If men will judge themselves and correct their errors, they can always escape the judgment of God. God gave Pharaoh an opportunity to stop oppressing His people, and let them be free to worship Him. Moses and Aaron were sent to Pharaoh with this word, "Let My people go, that they may hold a feast unto Me in the wilderness."

God is sending the same word today to this generation. He is saying, "Don't shut Me out of the training of your children; don't shut Me out of the media; don't silence Me in the civil courts; don't ignore Me in the decision-making process of government. Honor God and be just with one another." But the people of this generation have done exactly what the Psalmist prophesied. We have said, "Let us [Gentiles] break their [God and His Messiah] bands asunder, and cast away their cords from us" (Psalm 2:3).

In other words, "Let us throw off the ancient restraints of the Word of God, and be free from spiritual guidelines!" Many speculate about the role of the Church today. I watched a Protestant minister and a Catholic priest being interviewed about the duty of the Church in Central America. Both men maintained that the Church's responsibility is to become politically active. Certainly no one could deny that Moses was politically active.

But let us observe how he carried out his commission. To begin with, when Moses went back to Egypt to free Israel, he went under divine orders. Moreover, Moses carried with him only one agenda—the Word of God. Having delivered first of all the Word of God to the people, Moses then took the elders of Israel, and they appeared in Pharaoh's court with the same agenda—the Word of God.

The role of the minister is to make known the Word of God to the people. And if need be, to lead them into the courts of the world system with the same Word. Throughout his entire appeal, Moses never once altered his pattern nor his message. Going first to the people, delivering God's latest word, he would then go to Pharaoh, warning him of God's demands.

Politically speaking, the Word of God is the Church's agenda. Oh, how the Church needs to heed the warning here and cease compromising with the world. How we need to stand with resolve as the institutions of the world shake and crumble. How we need to let them fall, even when they are a part of our world. How we need to stop weeping over Pharaoh's crumbling system and start weeping over the constitution of God's kingdom system that lies in ruins in today's society.

When the hand of God began to fall upon the Egyptians, and the Egyptians in turn began to fall upon God's people, God's people panicked. They appeared before Moses and asked God to send judgment upon him. The people of God blamed Moses! The system was shaking, God's people were blamed, and they in turn blamed God's man! Yet, in His mercy, God sent them this word:

> Therefore say to the children of Israel: "I am the Lord; I will bring you out from under the burdens of the Egyptians, I will rescue you from their bondage, and I will redeem you with an outstretched arm and with great judgments. I will take you as My people, and I will be your God. Then you shall know that I am the Lord your God who brings you out from under the burdens of the Egyptians. And I will bring you into the land which I swore to give to Abraham, Isaac, and Jacob; and I will give it to you as a heritage: I am the Lord." (Exodus 6:6-8)

But do you know how Israel responded to this word from God? "...They hearkened not unto Moses." And do you know why they didn't listen? "...For anguish of spirit, and for cruel bondage" (Exodus 6:9).

That is, the people got so caught up in their misery that they took no comfort in the Word of God that promised to deliver them with "great judgments." For the Lord had said to Moses and the people:

> You shall speak all that I command you. And Aaron your brother shall speak to Pharaoh, that he must send the children of Israel out of his land. And I will harden Pharaoh's heart, and multiply My signs and My wonders in the land of Egypt. But Pharaoh will not heed you, so that I may lay My hand on

Egypt and bring My armies and My people, the children of Israel, out of the land of Egypt by great judgements. And the Egyptians shall know that I am the Lord, when I stretch out My hand on Egypt and bring out the children of Israel from among them. (Exodus 7:2-5)

Great judgments are determined for the earth during its last few years of Gentile government: great judgments on the world, great signs and wonders in the Church, and great deliverance for God's people both in the Church and the nation Israel. Those who understand this, will be able to stand faithful as Moses stood. Those whose hearts are still in the world will despair, as Israel anguished when their familiar world began to crumble, and the worldly— as Israel—will make some costly mistakes.

The First Contest

Having duly warned Pharaoh through His Word, God now enters into His very first contest with the powers of Satan. Taking his rod into Pharaoh's court—the same rod through which God would demonstrate His mighty signs and wonders—Moses proclaims God's second demand: "Let My people go that they may worship me." With that, Aaron cast down the rod and it became a serpent. With that, likewise, Pharaoh called his wise men who knew the occult arts, and they also cast down their rods and turned them into serpents.

Example #5:

In the last days, Satan-inspired men will have power to perform great miracles. This will be a key factor in the

43

great apostasy, or falling away from sound faith. This is a growing trend already in progress. Jesus said of this time, "Then if anyone says to you, 'Look, here is the Christ!' or 'There!' do not believe it. For false christs and false prophets will arise and show great signs and wonders, so as to deceive, if possible, even the elect" (Matthew 24:23,24).

We live in a supernatural, as well as natural, world. Anyone who tries to deny this fact is sorely misinformed. I watched an interview with a doctor who conducts what the interviewer called, "the most popular class at Harvard." The doctor's subject is children. In speaking of the dreams and desires of children around the world, the popular doctor had this to say, "All children are naturally spiritual."

"Parents who neglect the spiritual aspect of their children's lives hinder their ability to live bigger than themselves. They hinder their children's contributions to the lives of others. When children ask me what I think about God, I tell them, 'I'm still searching.'"

I do not know this doctor's personal beliefs, but his understanding of the reality of the supernatural is accurate. The Bible says man's life is as "the grass of the field which today is here and tomorrow is cast into the oven." Our natural lives are short-lived, but the Bible does not say we are grass—that once we die we are nothing. We are in fact eternal spirit beings, in natural bodies on a natural planet with supernatural powers all around us. When Pharaoh's men cast down their rods, they turned them into serpents. But given time, Aaron's rod swallowed up the rods of the magicians, and demonstrated to those who had eyes to see that not only are there two sources of supernatural powers on the earth but one Source is greater than the other. Signs and wonders will be demonstrated in these last days as the battle intensifies, but God's people will have the greater power.

And it shall come to pass in the last days, says God, that I will pour out of My Spirit on all flesh; your sons and your daughters shall prophesy, your young men shall see visions, your old men shall dream dreams. I will show wonders in heaven above and signs in the earth beneath: blood and fire and vapor of smoke. The sun shall be turned into darkness, and the moon into blood, before the coming of the great and notable day of the Lord. (Acts 2:17,19,20)

Example #6:

There is coming a great shaking in the world that will affect all people, including believers. It will begin just before the notable Day of the Lord. "...Ye are idle, ye are idle: therefore ye say, Let us go and do sacrifice to the Lord," Pharaoh said to those Israelites who wanted to take time from work to worship. "Go therefore now and work; for there shall no straw be given you, yet shall ye deliver the tale of bricks" (Exodus 5:17,18).

More than one contest is going to ensue as the day of "the coming exodus" draws near. Not only is God going to have a showdown with Satan, but He is also going to purify His people. Persecution is going to increase as the world becomes less and less respectful of religious people.

But the coming persecution of the Church and Israel has a divine mission. God is going to remove the "spots and wrinkles" from the lives of a compromised Church and an unbelieving Israel. He is preparing for Himself a virgin bride whose eyes will be only for the bridegroom, and a nation who will be a faithful host to their King.

Concerning the Church, Paul tells us that, "Christ...loved the church and gave himself for it, that He might sanctify and cleanse it with the washing of water by the word, that He might present it to Himself a glorious church, not having spot or wrinkle or any such thing, but that it should be holy and without blemish" (Ephesians 5:25-27).

Without "spot or wrinkle" means without blemish and marks of age. The Church has aging spots on its commission. Since the days of Israel, we have always had a difficult time staying pure, moisturized with the Word, and inflamed with zeal. Even when God pours out a refreshing revival upon us, we quickly turn that restoration into a restructuring of the old system, and before you know it, we have settled back into the world as just another institution.

Israel in Egypt had grown remarkably like Egypt. We know this from what happened once they started on their journey to Canaan. Idols, immorality, doubt and unbelief plagued them all the way. But God's Word declares that in the coming "exodus" He is going to shake the earth so thoroughly that this time nothing will be left standing that is not of Him, in the Church or outside it.

The Great Shaking

According to Scripture, a day is coming when "the kingdoms of this world will become the kingdoms of our God and of His Christ, and He shall reign forever and ever." The governments of this earth are destined for new leadership. Prior to this appointed time, however, the Bible says there will be three great events occurring worldwide:

- The great falling away
- The great shaking

• The great Day of the Lord

Before Jesus returns to earth as sovereign King, this earth is going to shake like a leaf under the weight of all mankind, strategically positioned to carry out its goals. The contest has already begun. Its momentum will intensify until our entire planet reeks with the sulphur of human nature erupting in total unrestraint. According to Scripture there will be three major teams in this life-and-death struggle: the religious apostate, the nation Israel, and the true Church of Jesus Christ, and it will all begin with the great falling away. The Apostle Paul wrote the following concerning this period of time:

> But relative to the coming of the Lord Jesus Christ, the Messiah, and our gathering together to meet Him, we beg you brothers, not to allow your minds to be quickly unsettled (shaken)...Let no one deceive or beguile you in any way, for that day will not come except the APOSTASY comes first—that is, unless the predicted great falling away of those who have professed to be Christians has come and the man of lawlessness (sin) is revealed.... (2 Thessalonians 2:1-3, Amplified)

The Great Falling Away

What is the great falling away? We have heard it mentioned. It remains theologically debatable. But taking the Bible literally, it simply means that before Jesus comes to earth again there is going to be a great falling away from biblical faith in God. Many religious people are going to defect, revolt and divorce themselves from the truth. This is what the word apostasy actually means in the original

47

Greek text: to defect, revolt, divorce itself. It describes a time when truth will be so thoroughly erased from society's religious, moral, and political dictionaries that real faith will lose its definition for most people.

Already, liberal theology and liberated morality have made themselves quite at home among twentieth-century Christianity. There is hardly a pastor who would deny that he has a three-part congregation: those who live like the world, those who think like the world, and those who struggle to overcome the world. Pure, biblical faith is undergoing one of the greatest persecutions ever leveled against it.

Throughout history, the faith of believers has endured wars, martyrdom, deportations, and mockery. It has known periods of moral decline and apathy—which opposition only tended to strengthen its determination. Not until the twentieth century has the Church been inundated with such a measure of seductive luxury and intellectual skepticism, that we have literally become a generation too sophisticated to believe in God. In writing to Timothy, the Apostle Paul lends some insight into this period of apostasy by saying,

Now the Spirit speaketh expressly, that in the latter times some shall depart from the faith, giving heed to seducing spirits, and doctrines of devils; speaking lies in hypocrisy; having their conscience seared with a hot iron; forbidding to marry, and commanding to abstain from meats, which God hath created to be received with thanksgiving of them which believe and know the truth" (1 Timothy 4:1-3).

If we take a minute to look at the symptoms of apostasy listed here, with minimal objectivity we will see that the very signals Paul exposed in his letter are common practices among many in the world today, as well as in the Church.

- Many will depart from the faith-denying the necessity of the new birth.

- Many will listen to seducing spirits—questioning the absolute authority of God's Word.

- People will give heed to doctrines of devils—seeking to unify all religions.

- There will be lying and hypocrisy—false teachers who are power-hungry and money oriented.

- People will become insensitive to right and wrong—compromising moral standards.

- They will be against marriage—anti-family, pro-abortion, career oriented.
- There will be a burst of dietary hang-ups—vegetarianism, anorexia, bulimia, excessive dieting and gluttony.

Does this description sound familiar? Even among believers you know, is it a familiar mind set? The symptoms are obvious, whether or not we choose to call them apostasy.

What a confused society we have become. We burn the midnight oil trying to find ways to save our young people from crime, drugs, and unwanted pregnancies, yet our afternoon television programs are filled with popular talk-show hosts interviewing the most immoral people they can possibly scrape out of the bottom of the trash cans. If intelligence were an earthquake, all the daytime soaps and most of the talk shows would not be able to cause a flicker on the Richter scale.

One has heard until he is sick that "what people do in privacy is no one's business." Does this mean that we may murder if we do it "in private"? Or rape? or rob? or plan espionage? If what one does in private costs the public thousands of dollars, as immorality does, is it still a private matter?

Technology has changed the safety we once enjoyed when it took ignorance longer to travel. Today we cannot only dial-a-prayer, but we have pornographic hot lines that will put a sizzling voice on the telephones for sex-crazed customers, and have public approval.

If the apostle Paul were writing in today's language he would say, "This is the plan that produces the great falling away:

- abandon biblical faith,
- do what pleases you,
- believe what you want."

The society that adopts this standard will prepare the way for the great shaking and Day of the Lord.

The Great Day of the Lord

At the present time, man is having his day. Satan and his deceived are riding high on the illusions of:

- secularism,
- immorality,
- materialism,
- pleasure-mania,
- and mind-powers.

But the time is coming when God says He is going to have His day:

> Behold, the Lord maketh the earth empty, and maketh it waste, and turneth it upside-down, and scat-

tereth abroad the inhabitants thereof. And it shall be, as with the people, so with the priest; as with the servant, so with his master; as with the maid, so with her mistress; as with the buyer, so with the seller; as with the lender, so with the borrower; as with the taker of usury, so with the giver of usury to him. ...The land shall be utterly spoiled: for the Lord hath spoke this word. (Isaiah 24:1-3)

In other words, there is coming a day when man's position, whether high or low, will not help him. Neither majority nor minority will have bearing on the Day of the Lord.

This is what Isaiah was trying to tell us when he said that laymen-clergy, employee-employer, buyer-seller, borrower—lender, and client—banker all stand on equal ground in the sight of God. In that day when God comes on the world scene as a refining fire, all human appointments will bow before "The President," and all power struggles will cease.

For the day of the Lord of hosts shall be upon every one that is proud and lofty, and upon every one that is lifted up; and he shall be brought low...The loftiness of man shall be bowed down, and the haughtiness of men shall be made low: and the Lord alone shall be exalted in that day. (Isaiah 2:12,17)

I am convinced that we are well into the social, moral and spiritual decline called the Great Falling Away. According to the Bible we are approaching the period of tribulation where the shaking will become increasingly noticeable. With rapid-fire succession, the Great Day of the Lord will then come.

The Bible declares, in at least twenty-five different references, that the earth is scheduled for such a day. It will be a shaking caused by the sin and rebellion of the human race. Yet, God is going to oversee the entire process to the very last item. When His purging has ceased, there will not be one single thing left standing that is not wholly dedicated to the principles of truth.

Listen to what God says is going to shake during this period of international upheaval. The heavens are going to shake, the earth is going to shake, everything is going to shake. Nothing and no one will be excluded from a thorough exposure of its true foundation.

The Heavens Will Shake

"Therefore, I will shake the heavens...," records Isaiah 13:13. Prior to the coming of Jesus to earth, cosmic changes will occur in space that have nothing to do with satellite probes. People will be astounded by changes in the sun, moon and stars. Periods of prolonged darkness will test the endurance of the mind, as well as strike fear in the hearts of the proudest unbeliever. It will be a paralyzing darkness that will bring a halt to all activities, as the darkness produced in Egypt.

The Earth Will Shake

"The earth shall reel to and fro like a drunkard, and shall be removed like a cottage; and the transgression thereof shall be heavy upon it; and it shall fall, and not rise again" (Isaiah 24:20).

This refers of course to the world system, not the earth itself. God is not going to lose one of His planets to sin. The present political, religious, and social systems that control this earth are going to stagger and collapse.

How utterly vain for humanistic people to think they can build "invincible institutions" on man-centered, mind-worshiping, immoral systems that ignore God. Every institution built by human logic is going to stagger like a drunk, when God removes His general grace from it. The hour when man arrives at the full potential of his own evil imagination, all common sense will have departed. Even now we are already experiencing a massive deficit of sound thinking.

Where can a person go today for sound advice and workable solutions to the issues that confront us daily? We gain energy—we pollute the air. We kill insects—we destroy the land. We manufacture more and more items—we pollute the waterways. We develop new educational methods—we destroy sound values.

My husband, Paul, recently spoke to the principal of a school, saying, "Your approach is totally humanistic and opposed to the principles of the Bible."

She responded, "That is absolutely correct. You run your church the way you want to, and I will run this school as I think best!" Yet that same school has all the modern plagues of drugs, venereal diseases, teenage pregnancies and various behavior problems.

The heavens are going to shake. The earth is going to shake. The governments of nations are going to shake.

The Governments Will Shake

"...distress of nations, with perplexity..." was the way Jesus said it. Policy deadlocks. The average person no longer knows which is the correct political posture for his government. Through the drama of the evening news, good and evil are brewed in the same pot and served in the best interest of public ratings. National loyalty is being supplanted with a global mentality, and a "new world order" has become the catch phrase.

The power to rule no longer rests in the hands of elected people. Writers, the media, and financial wizards now have the capability of molding public opinion in whatever direction they desire. Television has become the legal mouthpiece for unseen principalities and powers. There is a supernatural power in charge of the world today, just as there is a supernatural power in charge of the Church, and these two great powers are headed once again for Pharaoh's court.

It will be God's excuse for "the final removal and transformation of all that can be shaken...in order that what cannot be shaken may remain and continue..." (Hebrews 12:27, Amplified).

Although the Church has virtually overlooked it, there is a striking parallel between the plagues that struck Egypt and the plagues that John saw in the Revelation of the "last days." What God did in that period of "examples" with Israel and Egypt He is going to repeat in the days ahead. Without a doubt, this earth is destined to experience Pharaoh's plagues once again, while the Church and Israel get ready for the last great Exodus.

5

The Last Great Army

War is on the increase. According to one recent news report, the number of refugees world-wide has doubled since 1980. Technology is the answer to shorter wars, even safer wars, but not fewer wars. Wise King Solomon said it years ago, "There is a time for war." From now until the Millennium is that time. Rather than decreasing, wars and threats of wars will continue to multiply. God himself is raising up an army.

Man can talk of peace. We can fly back and forth in search of solutions, and we should. But when the King of the universe is raising up an army, there is going to be war. In every generation, the human race keeps repeating the same mistakes. They keep hoping to prevent permanent divorce between good and evil. But it's never going to happen. Good and evil are never going to coexist peacefully on this planet.

God will see to it that evil never gets control. Every time a new anti-God agenda comes on the scene, with some of the best minds in support of it, the matter comes to a head just as a boil ultimately festers into extinction.

Two middle-aged women sat in front of a large television audience of teen-agers, encouraging them to select their moral behavior the way one would select software for a computer—"Just pick whatever suits you." A young girl from the audience posed this question: "Do you think sex education in the schools helps to cut down on unwanted pregnancies and venereal disease?"

"Absolutely!" the female author responded. "The more we teach about sex the less problem we will have with it." But, can such an affirmation be validated? Anyone who is even vaguely aware of statistics over the past fifty years, knows that the fewest pregnancies outside marriage, and the fewest venereal diseases occurred when sex was not even a popular subject. The average junior high school student was not even thinking of birth control and venereal disease fifty years ago, for the simple reason they were being taught abstinence and chastity.

We use words as though they have the power to change the unwritten laws of creation. In a one-hour interview, the two aging talk show guests never once acknowledged even a remote possibility of such a thing as a moral law. Never once did they suggest to those young people that there are life-long consequences to countless intimate relationships. Never once did they mention the pains of premature responsibility for a family, financial burdens, lost careers, rejection and regrets. "Sex is a celebration of who we are!" concluded one of the two morally bankrupt sages.

And so it goes. With clever words, the world keeps trying to explain away the reasons for disagreements: object to nothing, agree to everything, and have peace.

Tell the Israelites that their role is to build cities, and they will stick peacefully to making bricks and pulling them through the desert sands. To the natural eye, Israel was nothing more than a bunch of slaves under the whip of Pharaoh. But do you know what they looked like to God? God said to Moses, "...Pharaoh shall not hearken unto you, that I may lay my hand upon Egypt, and bring forth mine armies..." (Exodus 7:4).

What did God call Israel? "Mine armies?" To God, Israel looked like an army! A "Passover" encounter with God makes soldiers out of slaves! Paul said to Timothy, "Endure hardness as a good soldier." God has always been in the business of raising up armies for the simple reason there are wars to be fought. A supernatural transformation took place on the day Israel killed the Passover lamb and applied its blood to the doorway of each Israelite home. The application of that blood brought down a power from heaven that not even the death angel could penetrate.

The Power of the Blood

I often wonder exactly what the death angel saw that night as he slithered along the narrow passageways in search of his prey. I wonder what he encountered as he approached the home of an Israelite. What did the blood of the lamb say to him—in the spirit realm—that caused him to back away and move on without a struggle? Does the blood have words of authority we don't know about, such as "Covenant Property?" Perhaps overlaying the blood was God's name—Jehovah! Were there legions of angels posted alongside each doorway? Where were Jesus and Satan at this time? We know that Jesus was not far away, as the Apostle Paul tells us that He was the cloud that protected Israel, the fire that guided them, and the manna that fed them in the desert. Were the Son of God and Satan walking the streets and sands of Egypt securing their legal positions, during that awesome night of battle?

The Day of the Lord

It was a time of battle. A great divorce was about to occur in the earth. God was about to separate His people from the unbeliever. It was the Day of the Lord. There were signs in the heavens; there were signs in the earth. The government of Egypt was in turmoil. The hand of God was set for a judgment that is to be repeated in the last days, when His wrath, not man's violence, will be demonstrated.

The Day of the Lord is not a day of man's violence against man. The first part of the seven last years of human history will be marked by the rise of the Antichrist, and his comet-like leap into fame, as negotiator for peace in the Middle East. This will be a period of approximately three and a half years, called "the beginning of sorrows" or "tribulation." This will be a time of man's violence against man. Then suddenly, when Antichrist's true colors surface, inhuman, demon-empowered violence will break out world-wide. Believers will be persecuted; Israel will be invaded, and many will be killed.

But the "Day of the Lord" is none of these events. God's day is a time of divine judgment on the wicked, the unbelievers, and all those who love and enjoy sin. The Day of the Lord will be a time that will bring "Egypt" to its knees.

People are inclined to talk about the end of human history as though we are destined for some unheard-of phenomenon, but God has always been quite open about His methods. Even though He is longsuffering, eventually God does two things regarding sin. First, He judges sin and second, He saves the repentant.

His methods have been demonstrated numerous times throughout history, and every demonstration of God falls into one of three categories: He gives signs in the heavens; He gives natural signs on earth; He gives supernatural signs in the spirit realm. Occasionally God brings the weight of all three to bear on the situation.

When God steps on the scales—heaven, earth, and the unseen powers all reflect His full weight. Thirty-five hundred years ago, God stepped on the scales in Egypt, and ten plagues rained down like fire. God is going to step on the scales in the last generation, and the whole world, but especially the Middle East, is going to taste the full course that was served on Egypt all over again.

In the midst of the fire, however, God is going to bring forth an army of warriors that will have the shout of a King among them. They will be royal people who have been purged, purified, and prepared to serve the Great God.

The disciples once posed this question to Jesus: "...Tell us, when will these things be? And what will be the sign of Your coming, and of the end of the age?" (Matthew 24:3).

Jesus answered their question by saying:

> ...Take heed that no one deceives you. For many
> will come in My name, saying, 'I am the Christ,' and
> will deceive many. And you will hear of wars and
> rumors of wars. See that you are not troubled; for all
> these things must come to pass, but the end is not yet.
> For nation will rise against nation, and kingdom
> against kingdom. And there will be famines, pesti-

lences, and earthquakes in various places. All these are the beginning of sorrows. (Matthew 24:4-8)

The Beginning of Sorrows

The beginning of Egypt's sorrows was natural disasters: The waters were turned into blood so that the fish died; the waters smelled and the people thirsted. Following this, the waters produced frogs in such abundance that they got into the people's houses, their beds, their kneading troughs, they even tormented their oxen, and in general made life unbearable. The dust of the ground turned into lice and covered both man and beast. Endless swarms of flies infested the houses and caused deadly diseases. Numerous diseases hit all livestock of the Egyptians and caused them to die. Locusts swooped down and ate their crops to the ground. Then suddenly there appeared a "sign in the heavens" and darkness covered the land. The Bible says Moses, "stretched forth his hand toward heaven; and there was a thick darkness in all the land of Egypt three days: They saw not one another, neither rose any from his place..." (Exodus 10:22-23).

This was a supernatural darkness, much like the effect of a three-day eclipse of the sun when there is not even a single reflection visible.

I once entered a cave where all light was extinguished. The feeling of total darkness, when one cannot even see his own hand, is frightening. Even though I was surrounded by other visitors to the cave, I had to consciously control my thoughts in order not to panic. Darkness is literally thick and suffocating when there is a total absence of light. Even Pharaoh's heart wavered in the pitch of God's supernatural demonstration.

With the weight of this plague Pharaoh was so tormented that he threatened Moses with death if he ever returned to his court again. It was in fact the end. The exodus was on the horizon. The darkness before the dawn had been enacted on the world stage as an example for the last generation.

And we who have arrived at the end need to remind ourselves that while the world cried out in anguish, Moses wrote that all the children of Israel "had light in their dwellings" (Exodus 10:23).

Remember, our key verse states that these things which happened to Israel were examples to us "on whom the ends of the world are come." And what is our example concerning the plague of darkness?

Example #7:

God will never turn out the lights on His faithful ones. Signs in the heavens will occur that will break the will of even the most arrogant. Yet, it will not strike fear in the hearts of those who are in fellowship with the God who is light in the dark places. As Corrie ten Boom, who suffered in a Nazi concentration camp, said, "No pit is too deep but He's deeper; no darkness so dark but He's light. Jesus alone will deliver, He will pierce the night."

John's Vision

Let us now compare what occurred in Egypt with the events the Apostle John saw when the heavens were opened to him and a view of the last generation appeared on the screen of time. The resemblance is remarkable. It takes the symbolism of the book of Revelation out of its mystical vocabulary and allows its descriptions to become as clear as "lice" and "frogs" and "supernatural darkness."

The last book in the Bible belongs in the Bible. Scholars sometime debate the validity of John's book, and allude to the possibility of its imposition on the main themes of love and forgiveness. Some spiritualize its symbolism as a metaphorical description of the Christian's struggles.

Revelation is in part expressed in the language of mystical symbolism, but I see it as being as literal as Israel in Egypt. John was a reporter. He was a Spirit-inspired reporter. But he was nonetheless a man who reported what he saw. Some of the things John saw he described in literal terms. Jesus, God, the throne of heaven with its senate, angels, animals, and colors—these John described as clearly as any modern day analyst would write for the daily news. The people and events of the future, however, John expressed in terms that described their character and work as opposed to their names and professional titles. Since the names of the places and people were unknown to him, John described what they would be like in appearance and function.

But if we can read Revelation as we read the book of Exodus; if we can envision an army of saints following Jesus down to the earth, as we envision the Israelites following Moses out of Egypt; if we can see God parting the heavens, as we see Him rolling back the walls of the Red Sea; if we can envision Jesus leading an army of raptured people—released from the bondages of mortality, as Israel was released from the whips of the Pharaoh; if we can eat the unleavened bread and drink the wine of the Lord's Supper, as Israel ate the Passover lamb; if we can endure the persecution of the ungodly and still cry out to God to be delivered; if we can believe that the God who sent Moses also sent Jesus; if we can believe that an army of Israelites marched through the lands of the pagans and nothing was able to stand in their way; if we can believe that these same people marched into Canaan and lived and prospered— then we can believe that God is raising up an army in the last days, who will be purified for a world-wide Passover celebration and Exodus unparalleled in history.

We can believe for a demonstration that will bring in the greatest harvest of souls the earth has ever seen, and we can believe that the Canaan Israel dreamed about will become a millennial reality.

I believe we should expect revival now, but the biggest revival of all time will not begin before the Second Coming of Jesus. The biggest battles are won when the full army moves in.

All of my life, I have heard that a great end-time army is coming in the last days that will bring about a world-wide revival and conversion of nations. Replacement theology (belief that the Church has replaced Israel and is destined to convert the nations in preparation for Jesus' coming), has spread in our generation on the projection that the Church will purify the earth for Jesus. But I simply cannot find evidence in Scripture to support such a claim. I believe such theology has its dates mixed up.

John saw the great army of Jesus coming with Him out of heaven prepared to make war on the nations. But why would Jesus be bringing an army to an earth that was already purified and converted?

If we set the dates in order, I believe we will be able to clear up a considerable number of misunderstandings regarding end-time events. Actually, the Apostle John has done a lot to assist us in clarifying the events surrounding the Second Coming of Jesus.

Beginning at verse nine in Revelation chapter 19, he writes:

> Then he said to me, 'Write: Blessed are those who are called to the marriage supper of the Lamb!' And he said to me, 'These are the true sayings of God.' Then I saw heaven opened, and behold, a white horse. And He who sat on him was called Faithful and True, and in righteousness He judges and makes war. And the armies in heaven, clothed in fine linen, white and clean, followed Him on white horses.
>
> Now out of His mouth goes a sharp sword, that with it He should strike the nations. And He Himself will rule them with a rod of iron. He Himself treads the winepress of the fierceness and wrath of Almighty God. Then I saw an angel standing in the sun; and he cried with a loud voice, saying to all the birds that fly in the midst of heaven, 'Come and gather together for the supper of the great God, that you may eat the flesh of kings, the flesh of captains, the flesh of mighty men, the flesh of horses and of those who sit on them, and the flesh of all people, free and slave, both small and great.' And I saw the beast, the kings of the earth, and their armies, gathered together to make war against Him who sat on the horse and against His army. Then the beast was captured, and with him the false prophet who worked signs in his presence, by which he deceived those who received the mark of the beast and those who worshiped his image.
>
> These two were cast alive into the lake of fire burning with brimstone. And the rest were killed with the sword which proceeded from the mouth of Him who sat on the horse. And all the birds were filled with their flesh. Then I saw an angel coming down from heaven, having the key to the bottomless pit and a

great chain in his hand. He laid hold of the dragon, that serpent of old, who is the Devil and Satan, and bound him for a thousand years; and he cast him into the bottomless pit, and shut him up, and set a seal on him, so that he should deceive the nations no more till the thousand years were finished. But after these things he must be released for a little while.

During the last seven years of human government, God is going to allow an evil plot to develop under a world-class leader called in Scripture "Antichrist." His plot will be to annihilate the statehood of Israel and kill the Jews. It will be another, but broader, version of Antiochus Epiphanes' desecration of the Temple and Hitler's holocaust.

As in the case of World War II, this political and military maneuver will involve all nations of the earth, yet with far more dramatic consequences. For the outcome of the final invasion of Israel will be the spark that will ignite a massive, earth-wide revival. It will be the time of the great ingathering of souls for which all heaven and earth have been waiting. When the army of the Lord, led by King Jesus, appears on this earth, there will be conversions of unparalleled proportions. The entire nation of Israel will be converted in one day.

And I will pour on the house of David and on the inhabitants of Jerusalem the Spirit of grace and supplication; then they will look on Me whom they have pierced; they will mourn for Him as one mourns for his only son, and grieve for Him as one grieves for a firstborn. In that day a fountain shall be opened for the house of David and for the inhabitants of Jerusalem, for sin and for uncleanness. (Zechariah 12:10; 13:1)

Five Egyptian cities will switch to the Hebrew language and worship the Messiah. Syria will experience phenomenal revival and conversions to Jesus, as will other Moslem states.

> In that day Egypt will be like women, and will be afraid and fear because of the waving of the hand of the Lord of hosts, which He waves over it. And the land of Judah will be a terror to Egypt; everyone who makes mention of it will be afraid in himself, because of the counsel of the Lord of hosts which He has determined against it. In that day five cities in the land of Egypt will speak the language of Canaan and swear by the Lord of hosts; one will be called the City of Destruction. In that day there will be an altar to the Lord in the midst of the land of Egypt, and a pillar to the Lord at its border. And it will be for a sign and for a witness to the Lord of hosts in the land of Egypt; for they will cry to the Lord because of the oppressors, and He will send them a Savior and a Mighty One, and He will deliver them. Then the Lord will be known to Egypt, and the Egyptians will know the Lord in that day, and will make sacrifice and offering; yes, they will make a vow to the Lord and perform it. And the Lord will strike Egypt, He will strike and heal it; they will return to the Lord, and He will be entreated by them and heal them. (Isaiah 19:16-22)

After Israel's personal and official acceptance of Messiah Yeshua, Egypt will follow suit and will turn to Jesus. As a result of their conversion, other Arab states will have their eyes opened to the truth, and a new trust will emerge in the Middle East that will spawn a trade policy that will demand a massive tri-state expressway.

> In that day will be a highway from Egypt to Assyria, and the Assyrian will come into Egypt, and the

Egyptian into Assyria, and the Egyptians will serve with the Assyrians. In that day Israel will be one of three with Egypt and Assyria, even a blessing in the midst of the land, whom the Lord of hosts shall bless, saying, 'Blessed is Egypt My people, and Assyria the work of My hands, and Israel My inheritance. (Isaiah 19:23-25)

At this time, when the Lord is enthroned in Israel, the immortal Church—the last great army—will go out to rule and reign under the government of King Jesus, and Israel will pick up her ancient mandate to be a spiritual light to the nations:

Now therefore, if you will indeed obey My voice and keep My covenant, then you shall be a special treasure to Me above all people; for all the earth is Mine. And you shall be to Me a kingdom of priests and a holy nation. These are the words which you shall speak to the children of Israel. (Exodus 19:5-6)

But this takes us ahead of the story. Before the Millennium there must be an exodus. This is what we are going to look at in the next two chapters—Israel rescued at the closing seconds of the Great Tribulation and the Day of the Lord, and the Church raptured some time prior to the rescue.

6

The Church Raptured

Anyone who declares that he can pinpoint the Rapture of the Church deserves to be taken lightly. The Bible never looks so big as when one reads the prophetic literature regarding the end times. Yet, I do believe we can have a general idea of the time frame of this and other related events.

Israel did not know the exact moment of their exodus from Egypt, but they did know it was near enough to feel its breath, when they were told to keep on their clothes, have their feet shod and their food prepared for traveling.

The "beginning of sorrows" had occurred when a Pharaoh came to power who did not know Joseph. Gradually the pressure began to increase until it had finally reached the point of persecution. It was during this time that God appeared to Moses and said, "Now therefore, behold, the cry of the children of Israel has come to Me, and I have also seen the oppression with which the Egyptians oppress them. Come now, therefore, and I will send you to Pharaoh that you may bring My people, the children of Israel, out of Egypt" (Exodus 3:9,10).

The Bible tells us that a similar day is coming when God will say to Jesus, "The times of the Gentiles is fulfilled. The Church is prepared for its exodus. Go and get them!"

> For the Lord Himself will descend from heaven with a shout, with the voice of an archangel, and with the trumpet of God. And the dead in Christ will rise first. Then we who are alive and remain shall be caught up together with them in the clouds to meet the Lord in the air. And thus we shall always be with the Lord (1 Thessalonians 4:16-17)

> But concerning the times and the seasons, brethren, you have no need that I should write to you. For you yourselves know perfectly that the day of the Lord so comes as a thief in the night. For when they cry, 'Peace and safety!' then sudden destruction comes upon them, as labor pains upon a pregnant woman. And they shall not escape. But you, brethren, are not in darkness, so that this Day should overtake you as a thief.....For God did not appoint us to wrath, but to obtain salvation through our Lord Jesus Christ. (1 Thessalonians 5:1-4,9)

The Beginning of Sorrows

The Rapture of the Church should come as no surprise to those who make a point to understand the signs of the times. Jesus told us clearly how to discern the calendar. The clock hangs in Israel, the ticking of the second hand is moving to bring the Antichrist into a scenario of:

- Increasing wars and international unrest,
- Increasing famine, earthquakes and floods,
- Increasing pestilence and outbreaks of disease,
- Increasing persecution of saints and cosmic disturbances.

This is "the beginning of sorrows." Revelation 5 describes it this way: John the greatly loved disciple of Jesus was exiled to the island of Patmos for his faith. The year was about A.D. 96, approximately sixty-three years after the ascension of Jesus back to heaven. As John was "in the Spirit," that is, in total union with the Holy Spirit, wholly yielded to Him on the Lord's day, the curtain of time between heaven and earth was lifted. Past, present and future became one visible scene.

Looking into heaven, John saw God seated with a book in His hand that was sealed with seven seals. A strong angel stepped forward and with a loud voice proclaimed, "Who is worthy to open the book, and to loose the seals thereof?" (Revelation 5:2).

By the word "worthy" he did not mean "good enough" but powerful enough to break the seals, as we shall see in the scene that follows. After a period of great sadness, when it appeared to John that "no man was found worthy to open and read the book," one of the redeemed elders said to John, "Weep not: behold, the Lion of the tribe of Judah, the Root of David, hath prevailed [conquered, gotten the victory, overcome] to open the book, and to loose the seals thereof" (Revelation 5:5).

John records:

> And I looked, and behold, in the midst of the throne
> and of the four living creatures, and in the midst of

71

the elders, stood a Lamb as though it had been slain, having seven horns and seven eyes, which are the seven Spirits of God sent out into all the earth. Then He came and took the scroll out of the right hand of Him who sat on the throne. Now when He had taken the scroll, the four living creatures and the twenty-four elders fell down before the Lamb, each having a harp, and golden bowls full of incense, which are the prayers of the saints. And they sang a new song, saying: "You are worthy to take the scroll, and to open its seals; for You were slain, and have redeemed us to God by Your blood out of every tribe and tongue and people and nation, and have made us kings and priests to our God; and we shall reign on the earth" (Note their destination is earth). (Revelation 5:6-10)

The seal was the ancient way of validating a document. In Roman law a testament or will was sealed with seven seals by seven witnesses. In divine terms seven means completion. The document in Jesus' hand was the complete record of the final days of time, and it was fully stamped with seven seals.

The Seals

I watched as the Lamb opened the first of the seven seals. Then I heard one of the four living creatures say in a voice like thunder, "Come!" I looked, and there before me was a white horse! Its rider held a bow, and he was given a crown, and he rode out as a conqueror bent on conquest. (Revelation 6:1-2)

The Book of Revelation is written in a language of both natural and supernatural terms, as well as symbolism. The horses that are loosed with the breaking of the first four seals are actually four "spirits or winds" that stand in the presence of God. Zechariah spoke of them this way:

> Then I turned and raised my eyes and looked, and behold, four chariots were coming from between two mountains, and the mountains were mountains of bronze. With the first chariot were red horses, with the second chariot black horses, with the third chariot white horses, and with the fourth chariot dappled horses—strong steeds. Then I answered and said to the angel who talked with me, "What are these, my lord?" And the angel answered and said to me, "These are four spirits of heaven, who go out from their station before the Lord of all the earth." (Zechariah 6:1-5)

Man is not the center of creation—God is. Man is only one of many creatures designed and given life by God. Heaven has many creatures far greater in power and intellect than fallen man. The "four horses" John saw are four "beings." They are referred to several times throughout the Scriptures. Jesus himself spoke of these horses as beings having a role in the end-times.

"And He will send His angels with a great sound of a trumpet, and they will gather together His elect from the four winds, from one end of heaven to the other" (Matthew 24:31).

The "four winds" of God are not simply the oxygen mixture you and I breathe to stay alive, but they are "beings" of powerful transportation and mission. Zechariah referred to them as beings that patrol the earth and report to God about the human condition. (See Zechariah 1:8-11.)

Therefore, John's vision of Jesus breaking the seals on the divine document in God's hand, was actually Jesus releasing four intense and powerful "beings" to carry out His predestined judgments on a world system of sin, greed, immorality and lawlessness.

Remember, nothing and no one, including Satan, can do anything without God's permission. In the end-days, God is going to grant Satan permission to do a quick but destructive sweep of deception across planet earth for the purpose of exposing the hearts of men. The breaking of the seals is the birth of such a sweep.

The First Seal Releases a White Horse

The release of the White Horse from God will grant Satan permission to bring his "imitation christ" to the political arena. Anti means in place of. In the last seven years of human government, the Antichrist—a world class leader— is coming to the forefront of Middle-Eastern politics with supernatural solutions to the Arab-Israeli conflict. He will be the false "prince of peace." Like a comet, he will come on the scene and soar as Alexander the Great soared, quickly and gloriously.

The Second Seal Releases a Red Horse

The release of the Red Horse will give Satan permission to do legal slaughter. "To him was given a large sword" John writes. The word used here for sword describes the short Roman sword that brought about violent deaths and abuses by the authorities.

If we go back to Israel when the Hebrews were in the land of Egypt, we will see how this parallels precisely what happened to them, as the day of their exodus drew near. Remember we learned that "taskmasters" were placed over the Hebrews. They were "authorities" sent to browbeat and break them apart. God instituted civil government as a way of maintaining cohesive law and order according to justice. But history shows us that there have always been leaders who took their liberties as a right to enforce injustice.

With the breaking of the Second Seal, abuse of authority will sweep the nations. Some will be chaotic and spread fear, some will take the form of subtle abuse and work covertly to manipulate the people into cooperation.

The Third Seal Releases a Black Horse

The breaking of the Third Seal releases a rider on a Black Horse, who carries a pair of scales in his hand. What he brings is famine.

The present projection for this decade is being stated regularly in numerous world reports: Millions will starve in Africa within the next few years. The number in the Far East who have already died from floods and monsoons will increase. Cholera outbreaks in South America and world-wide increase of AIDS show a pattern of increasing plagues. Something the world has never faced is the fact that no disease-causing organism has ever been eradicated. They are merely brought under control. Any plague that has ever occurred is subject to break out again. Only recently, a report came out that tuberculosis is again on the rise. With the release of the Black Horse, the earth will see an outbreak of many plagues we no longer consider a threat. With the spread of famine will come the spread of disease.

I listened to a lecturer on economics award the future to the nations that are "technologically aggressive." He declared that American farmland will have little value in the future, compared to its value in the past. "The future belongs to the aggressive technology-based nations," he said. But the balance to this point of view is food. Who will feed the people? As great as they are, no one has yet made a digestible computer that will fill empty stomachs and bring rain to drought-stricken wastelands. Famine is bigger than technology, and when the Black Horse arrives, proud men are going to realize it.

The Fourth Seal Releases the Pale Horse

The rider of the Pale Horse is named Death and Hades. This rider is given power over a fourth part of the earth "to kill by sword, famine, plague, and by the wild beasts of the earth" (Revelation 6:8).

War is never simply men shooting at one another. It is a unit of destruction that always carries with it famine, disease and displacement. With the breaking of the Fourth Seal wars will increase significantly. Regional instability in hot spots such as the Middle East will pose a constant threat, and general international unrest will hinder the flow of goods. The result will be warehouses of plenty in a world of want and need—the "beginning of sorrows."

The breaking of these first four seals represents what Jesus called unprecedented troubles. It is more or less the first 3 1/2 years of the seven final years described in Scripture as the Tribulation. Tribulation is that period when the earth goes into labor to bring forth its solution to sin and death. It is a pain that will alternate between joy and sorrow, in the sense that the birth of a child arrives with tears and laughter. Out of intense pain, repentance will come forth unto life, and 1,000 years of peaceful productivity will be set to overtake the warring nature of man, and the lion will indeed lie down with the lamb.

When the disciples posed the question to Jesus: "What shall be the sign of your coming and the end of the world?" Jesus answered His disciples this way,

> Take heed that no one deceives you. For many will come in My name, saying, 'I am the Christ,' and will deceive many. And you will hear of wars and rumors of wars. See that you are not troubled; for all these things must come to pass, but the end of the world is not yet. For nation will rise against nation, and kingdom against kingdom. And there will be famines, pestilences, and earthquakes in various places. All these are the beginning of sorrows.

The Great Tribulation

The plagues of Egypt are destined to be experienced again on this earth. All nations are going to be touched by them. As we learned from Egypt, however, the contest between God and Satan only intensifies with time. The beginning "birth pangs" quickly developed into life and death contractions. Persecution and inhuman treatment soon followed the "beginning of sorrows" for Israel, once Pharaoh had set his face against them.

Jesus said,

> Then they will deliver you up to tribulation and kill you, and you will be hated by all nations for My name's sake. And many will be offended, will betray one another, and will hate one another. Then many false prophets will rise up and deceive many. And because lawlessness will abound, the love of many will grow cold. But he who endures to the end shall

be saved. And this gospel of the kingdom will be preached in all the world as a witness to all the nations, and then the end will come. (Matthew 24:9-14)

Lawlessness occurs when the courts no longer enforce wise standards for human behavior. A nation without a standard is a nation on its way to lawlessness and chaos. The period of time following the "beginning of sorrows" is called in Scripture the "Great Tribulation." It is that period of approximately two to three and a half years when people determined to hold up the standard of God will undergo their greatest opposition.

In one week of daytime television in America, among dozens of immoral and violent programs, two men married each other before the cameras and a female author begged to describe the intimate lifestyle of lesbianism, which she practices. The day has arrived when the minds and very core of sound thinking people is being vexed and tormented by a constant flood of moral standards comparable to those of Sodom and Gomorrah. In the major city where we live, it is a very normal part of our day to be sworn at violently by other drivers. Even the children on the summer baseball teams are allowed to use profanity against each other.

Pharaoh's hand hardened against Moses. But as it did, Moses strengthened himself in miracle demonstrations of God. The more hardships Pharaoh poured on God's people, the greater the difference God made between His people and the ungodly. I believe the same will occur in the last days. The Church will experience once again the miracle power of God in mortal combat with the forces of hell.

The Fifth Seal Loosed Persecution of the Saints & Martyrdom

Paul was beheaded, Peter was crucified, Andrew was skinned alive, James was killed with Herod's sword, and Stephen was stoned. Hebrews 11 gives an impressive list of notables who suffered greatly for the gospel's sake. Only those who have truly released this world are able to stand when the world is brought into the courtroom of God's interrogation concerning its career of sin. But believers need to bear in mind that the Word of God will still work for them in tribulation as it does in times of plenty. His promises apply to the end-days as much as they do to any other time.

Abounding favor from God is always available when sin shows its greatest strength. When Paul wrote the famous line, "Where sin abounded, grace did much more abound" (Romans 5:20), he meant to remind us that in the hour when human plight sinks lowest, the favor of God will increase to its highest potential.

To "abound" literally means to have in excess, to become too great, to be over. Therefore, in that day when human nature is turned loose and the authorities only enforce lawlessness, the people of God will actually have an excess of power available to meet their challenges. It will be a time when heroes are made for the libraries of the Millennium. It will be a day when God's people will literally overcome impossible situations—to the point of excessive victories.

Yes, some will be martyred and go into the presence of God in preparation for the Second Coming of Jesus. But others will prevail and be alive for the Rapture of the saints! The key word is to "endure" and not to despair. Understand, however, that the word endure does not mean to grit your teeth and hold on, but to stand up and move forward. Persecution is a time to move forward. The Church has always done some of its best growing when persecution was at its height.

The Sixth Seal is Loosed

When the Sixth Seal is broken, the heavens will begin to talk in a language that will drive even the bravest men to the mountains, looking for cover. "And the kings of the earth, the great men, every slave and every free man, hid themselves in the caves and in the rocks of the mountains, and said to the mountains and rocks, Fall on us and hide us from the face of Him who sits on the throne and from the wrath of the Lamb!'" (Revelation 6:15-16).

For those who believe in the pre-tribulation rapture of the 1 Church, the only believers present on earth at this point (thirty-one and half years into the last seven years of tribulation), will be those who are converted after the rapture of the Church.

For those who hold to the mid-tribulation rapture, the breaking of the Sixth Seal sets the stage for the possible departure of the Church at any moment prior to the wrath of God.

For those who believe in the post-tribulation rapture, the Church will experience the entire seven-years tribulation, overcoming and rising to meet the Lord in the air at the moment He descends to earth. In all fairness, there are Scriptures and able scholars to support all three positions. The common factor and most significant to keep in mind is the agreement of all three, and that is the certainty of the rapture.

The word rapture comes from the Latin *rapere*, meaning rapid. Paul wrote,

> For the Lord himself will descend from heaven with a shout, with the voice of an archangel, and with the trumpet of God. And the dead in Christ will rise first. Then we who are alive and remain shall be caught up together with them in the clouds to meet the Lord in the air. And thus we shall always be with the Lord. (1 Thessalonians 4:16-17)

The term "caught up" means to carry off hastily. The Latin translation of this term is rapture. Jesus will descend from—leave heaven to meet us in the air. At the rapture, are we going to be called to heaven to meet Jesus, or shall we meet Him only in the air?

One day soon it will become clear. One thing is certain, this "catching up" will happen, not so that we may remain in the heavens with the Lord forever, but so that He may prepare us to return with him as a part of His victorious army, headed for the Marriage Supper of the Lamb.

Thirty-five hundred years ago, Israel sat like a watchdog behind the blood-stained doorways of their homes, dressed and ready to march on a moment's notice. The cries of Egypt could be heard throughout the still night air of the desert as the death angel collected his precious booty. Suddenly, as the sun began to rise above the glimmering sands of slavery, a trumpet blast was sounded and God caught up a nation of men, women, and children and headed them for the promised land. History records that Israel marched out of Egypt a free people.

It is going to happen again? Who but God could design such a masterpiece that thirty-five hundred years or so after the first exodus, His Church would find itself standing watch under the protective blood of the Lamb, overcoming the persecutions, and making itself ready on a moment's notice, to hear the trumpet call to join the procession to the same land of Canaan that He first called Israel?

As surely as Israel was released from the strong arm of Pharaoh, the Church is as certainly going to be caught up in the air to meet Jesus. Before the "wrath of God" is revealed against sin, the dead in Christ will have their bodies resurrected from the ground, the Church will be changed from mortal to immortal, and we will depart this earth for a brief period of time, while God finishes His contest with Satan and completes His work with the nation of Israel. This is the period of the opening of the Seventh Seal.

This is what we are going to look at in our next chapter. Israel is destined for another exodus from annihilation.

7

Israel Rescued

Israel. Dr. C.M. Ward has called her "a bastion in the midst of envy." (*Christ for the Nations Magazine*, March, 1991.) In size and in number, she is among the least. Yet in assignment, Israel is a bastion—a fortification, a bulwark within the family of nations. Not that she has lived up to her assignment. Clearly she has not. This is her problem. Will Israel ever live up to her divine responsibility? Absolutely. This is her salvation.

In proportion to the entire land mass of planet earth, Israel will never be large. Her borders were fixed by God 4,000 years ago when He covenanted with Abraham, "... Unto thy seed have I given this land, from the river of Egypt unto the great river, the river Euphrates" (Genesis 15:18). The land of Israel will eventually extend from Egypt to Iraq. But her influence during the Millennium is going to be much larger than this, even world-wide.

From envy to honor, the time is coming when the nations of earth will send ambassadors to Israel seeking the wisdom that will flow out of its government, just as ancient kings went to Solomon for the same reason . According to Ezekiel, Jerusalem, the capital city of Israel and of the whole earth, will measure "twelve miles square."

That is 144,000 square miles. In size and beauty, in political stature and moral example, Jerusalem will be appropriate for a world capital. (See Ezekiel 45:6.)

In Israel will be the answers, the solutions, for which all leaders now search. "Thus saith the Lord of hosts; In those days it shall come to pass, that ten men shall take hold out of all languages of the nations, even shall take hold of the skirt of him that is a Jew, saying 'We will go with you: for we have heard that God is with you'" (Zechariah 8:23).

And where will they be going?

Two thousand years ago "wise men" went to Jerusalem in search of a king. This time they are going to find Him, not in Bethlehem, but ruling from a temple-sanctuary complex, whose exact measurements were given to Israel 2,600 years ago.

Sitting in Babylonian captivity about 600 B.C., Ezekiel, the prophet had a vision from God, in which he was brought by the Spirit to a future date when Messiah would be sitting on a throne in Jerusalem. This is what he wrote:

> In the visions of God He took me into the land of Israel and set me on a very high mountain; on it toward the south was something like the structure of a city. He took me there, and behold, there was a man whose appearance was like the appearance of bronze. He had a line of flax and a measuring rod in his hand, and he stood in the gateway. And the man said to me, "Son of man, look with your eyes and hear with your

ears, and fix your mind on everything I show you; for you were brought here so that I might show them to you. Declare to the house of Israel everything you see." (Ezekiel 40: 2-4)

What Ezekiel saw were the exact dimensions of the Millennial Sanctuary from which Jesus will rule the earth from Jerusalem. He saw new laws instituted (Ezekiel 43:10-12), new land divisions to the twelve tribes of Israel (Ezekiel 45:9; 47:13-48:7; 48:23-29), new worship in Israel (Ezekiel 45:13-46:24), new and eternal Jerusalem, and many other details regarding Israel during the Millennium. The vision recorded by Ezekiel (chapters 40-48), was a complete architectural rendering of God's future plans for the nation, the land and the individual tribes of the natural descendants of Abraham's son, Isaac. The things Ezekiel saw were not vague nor symbolic, they were not suggestive nor sketchy. God did not summon Ezekiel until a complete draft was off the drawing board and had passed through His hands for a final perusal. What the angel showed the prophet was the same set of drawings an architect hands the contractor before he begins a new project. He was in fact instructed to "declare all that you see to the house of Israel" (Ezekiel 40:4).

Imagine all the years the world has questioned Israel's right to exist as a nation, and the Church has questioned if Israel still has a relationship with God—when God has a complete architectural rendering of their land and national future preserved right in the middle of the Bible!

What architect would draw up an elaborate set of plans and dispatch them by a special courier, when he had no intention of building his project? Certainly such behavior would not be fitting to the character of God.

85

After describing the millennial temple to Ezekiel, the Messiah said to him, "...Son of man, the place of my throne and the place of the soles of my feet, where I will dwell in the midst of the children of Israel for ever, and my holy name, shall the house of Israel no more defile [contaminate]..." (Ezekiel 43:7).

And then Messiah goes on to explain how Israel contaminated God's name through idolatry and murders of kings and prophets, during their first attempt to live in relationship with the holy God.

"Thou son of man, shew the house to the house of Israel, that they may be ashamed of their iniquities: and let them measure the pattern" (Ezekiel 43:10).

In other words, first let Israel repent, and then let them get ready to build!

With that, the Messiah then showed Ezekiel the pattern of His future house, and all the ordinances that would be conducted in it including the sin offering as Israel once sacrificed for their sins. Yes, throughout the Millennium, Israel will be offering sacrifices to God as a reminder to themselves of the sacrifice Messiah paid for their salvation. (See Ezekiel 43:18-27.)

The Church of present believing Jews and Gentiles has already accepted the sacrificial death and shed blood of Jesus. We acknowledge that "without the shedding of blood there is no remission of sins." In the Millennium, the nation Israel will acknowledge the same. "And so all Israel will be saved, as it is written: 'The Deliverer will come out of Zion, and He will turn away ungodliness from Jacob'" (Romans 11:26).

Israel is set for an exodus greater than that of Egypt. At the opening of the Seventh Seal, when the wrath of God is revealed from heaven, Israel is going to encounter a limited number of days—less than three and one-half years—when she will undergo her greatest testing and her deepest purification.

It will be a day worse than the domination of Antiochus who sacrificed a pig in the most Holy Place, and "according to the decree, they put to death the women who had their children circumcised, and their families and those who circumcised them; and they hung the infants from their mothers' necks" (From *The Apocrypha*, 1 Maccabees 1:60-61). It will be worse than the days when Hitler herded mothers and their two million young into the gas chambers of Europe. Jesus said of the persecution:

For then there will be great tribulation, such as has not been since the beginning of the world until this time, no, nor ever shall be. And unless those days were shortened, no flesh would be saved; but for the elect's sake those days will be shortened. [For Israel's sake the days will be limited.] (Matthew 24:21,22)

Daniel (9:27) wrote of the coming evil pharaoh—Antichrist—that, "in the midst of the week he shall cause the sacrifice and the oblation to cease." That is, he will break the peace treaty with Israel at the halfway point of the last seven years of Gentile history, and forbid them to exist as a Jewish state. Halfway into the seven-year Middle East peace treaty, the Antichrist will outlaw the practice of Judaism—as did the Syrian, Antiochus Epiphanes—and events around the temple area in Jerusalem will advance quickly toward Armageddon and the great Day of the Lord.

Evidence does not convince me whether the Antichrist—Satan's answer to Christ—will walk into a Jewish temple building and declare himself the prince of peace, or if he will simply set up his headquarters on the ancient temple grounds, where God's house once stood and where the Jews presently pray beside the Wailing Wall.

Satan knows the significance of this place. He understands that this spot has been selected by God as the location of Messiah's Millennial Sanctuary. That's why he has a mosque located there now. But to change that mosque for the Antichrist's headquarters will constitute an unprecedented act of defiance in the spirit realm. It will be in real terms—the ultimate challenge.

The spirit world sees the temple mount as the undisputed location for the future world capital buildings. Whoever controls that spot controls the world system. Until the temple area is settled, the Middle East will know no peace. The question of who will rule the world must be settled at the ancient temple mount. This point above all others is the catalyst for Armageddon. God has selected this particular sight for Messiah's headquarters. The plans have been drawn up. The architectural renderings have been approved. With the breaking of the Seventh Seal, Jesus and His hosts will engage Satan and his hosts for a final showdown. Pharaoh and Moses will once again be standing eye to eye.

The Day of the Lord (Breaking of Seventh Seal)

For clarity's sake take a look at the seals once more: John saw Jesus take a book from God's hand that had seven seals on it. The book contained a description of the seven final years of human history as we know it.

As Jesus began to break the seals, events began to occur here on earth between the Spirit of God and the spirit of evil.

- With the First Seal came the Antichrist on to the political scene, taking dominion through false diplomacy in the Middle East.

- With the Second Seal came war.

- With the Third Seal came famine.

- With the Fourth Seal came disease and death resulting from wars.

- With the Fifth Seal came persecution of believers— both the Church and the nation Israel.

- With the Sixth Seal came cosmic disturbances, prolonged darkness and signs in the heavens— with increased earthquakes on the earth.

John writes of this time that the heavens will roll back like a scroll and men will run to the mountains looking for safety, "for the great day of his [God's] wrath is come: and who shall be able to stand?" (Revelation 6:17).

At this time God will send an angel to place His mark on 144,000 Jews from the twelve tribes of Israel and the Church will be raptured. (See Revelation 7:1-8.)

> After these things I looked, and behold, a great multitude which no one could number, of nations, tribes, peoples, and tongues, standing before the throne and before the Lamb, clothed with white robes, with palm branches in their hands, and crying out with a loud voice, saying, "Salvation belongs to our God who sits on the throne, and to the Lamb!" And I said to him,

"Sir, you know." So he said to me, "These are the ones who came out of the great tribulation, and washed their robes and made them white in the blood of the Lamb. (Revelation 7:9-10,14)

The Day of the Lord—the Wrath Revealed

Then comes the opening of the Seventh Seal and the Day of the Lord begins. This period of time is divided into fourteen periods—seven trumpets and seven vials. These represent months or varying periods of time that altogether do not exceed forty-two months. (See Revelation 13:5.)

Seven trumpets are sounded in heaven and seven vials are broken. With the sound of each of these actions in heaven a judgment falls on the earth.

Seven Trumpets

- First trumpet: hail, fire and blood rain from heaven.

- Second trumpet: A burning meteor hits the ocean and one-third of sea life dies.

- Third trumpet: One-third of water becomes polluted.
- Fourth trumpet: One-third of the planet becomes darkened, and days are cut short by one-third.

- Fifth trumpet: Demons loosed out of hell sting men (except those Jews sealed by God).

- Sixth trumpet: Four demons loosed out of the

Euphrates river kill one-third of people (of Middle East).

● Seventh trumpet: Antichrist makes war on Israel (Revelation 11:15 and Chapter 12). But God prepares a place of escape for a remnant.

Awake, O sword, against My Shepherd, against the Man who is My Companion," says the Lord of hosts. "Strike the Shepherd, and the sheep will be scattered; then I will turn My hand against the little ones. And it shall come to pass in all the land," says the Lord, "that two-thirds in it shall be cut off and die, but one-third shall be left in it: I will bring the one-third through the fire, will refine them as silver is refined, and test them as gold is tested. They will call on My name, and I will answer them, I will say, 'This is My people'; and each one will say, 'The Lord is my God.'"(Zechariah 13:7-9)

Zechariah describes Israel's position in the day of wrath this way:

Behold, I will make Jerusalem a cup of drunkenness to all the surrounding peoples, when they lay siege against Judah and Jerusalem. And it shall happen in that day that I will make Jerusalem a very heavy stone for all peoples; all who would heave it away will surely be cut in pieces though all nations of the earth are gathered against it. It shall be in that day that I will seek to destroy all the nations that come against Jerusalem. And I will pour on the house of David and on the inhabitants of Jerusalem the Spirit of grace and supplication; then they will look on Me whom they have pierced; they will mourn for

Him as one mourns for his only son, and grieve for Him as one grieves for a firstborn. In that day there shall be a great mourning in Jerusalem. In that day a fountain shall be opened for the house of David and for the inhabitants of Jerusalem, for sin and for uncleanness. (Zechariah 12:2-3, 9-11;13:1)

Seven Vials

Great persecution, great purging, great purification—this is the destiny of Israel during the political and cosmic upheavals of the last three and a half years of history. Following the blowing of the Seven Trumpets of Judgment on the earth comes the rapid-fire breaking of the Seven Vials, with an amazing resemblance to the plagues that fell on Pharaoh's Egypt:

- First Vial: Sores on the ungodly who follow the Antichrist.

- Second Vial: Sea turns to blood.

- Third Vial: Fresh water turns to blood.

- Fourth Vial: Scorching heat comes from the sun. Perhaps the ozone layer will be destroyed allow ing the ultraviolet rays of the sun to burn man's skin.

- Fifth Vial: Dense darkness falls on Antichrist's king dom. This will be a supernatural darkness that will literally touch men's bodies and torture their minds.

> Then the Lord said to Moses, "Stretch out your hand toward heaven, that there may be darkness over the land of Egypt, darkness which may even be felt." So Moses stretched out his hand toward heaven, and there was thick darkness in all the land of Egypt three days. They did not see one another; nor did anyone rise from his place for three days. But all the children of Israel had light in their dwellings. (Exodus 10:21-23)

- Sixth Vial: Euphrates River dries up, releasing three unclean spirits (powers) in the Middle East which helps to draw Israel and the nations to Armaged don to battle.

- Seventh Vial: In the Middle East great earthquakes will hit and hailstones weighing one hundred and fourteen pounds each will fall.

> Now the great city was divided into three parts, and the cities of the nations fell. And great Babylon was remembered before God, to give her the cup of the wine of the fierceness of His wrath. (Revelation 16:19)

The end of man's day has finally arrived. The Day of the Lord is begun. The stage is the Middle East. All nations are involved—even as they are today by international military representation. But the performance will take place in the Middle East where Satan hopes to stake a permanent claim on God's "holy site" for His Son's Sanctuary. Nations play the human roles in this final drama, but the principalities and powers of the heavenly regions are the true source behind the conflict. The Seventh Vial releases the final struggles that are set to occur as the Antichrist and his allies try to annihilate the Jews once and for all—even to the point of challenging the Son of God as He comes to rescue Israel.

Satan has been after the Messianic nation since the day God announced that the seed of a woman would be his downfall. In Genesis 3:15 God made it clear that the birth of a baby was His answer to the human dilemma. Through Pharaoh, Satan went after God's first deliverer, Moses. But God hid the child right in Pharaoh's court, and not only did Moses escape Pharaoh's death sentence, but Pharaoh financed the education and training of God's man! Yes, Satan is more clever than fallen man, but he is no match for God!

Even so, in the great Day of the Lord, as he did in Egypt, Satan is going after Israel and God's "Deliverer" once again. We can read about it in John's revelation:

> Now a great sign appeared in heaven: a woman clothed with the sun, with the moon under her feet, and on her head a garland of twelve stars. Then being with child, she cried out in labor and in pain to give birth. And another sign appeared in heaven behold, a great, fiery red dragon having seven heads and ten horns, and seven diadems on his heads. (Revelation 12:1-3)

The "sun-clothed woman" is national Israel. (See Genesis 37:9-11.) The "great red dragon having seven heads, and ten horns and seven crowns" represents Satan and his Gentile empires that have attacked Israel since God's Messianic plan of salvation was declared.

The seven heads represent the seven empires that have risen throughout Gentile history: Egypt, Assyria, Babylon, Medo-

Persia, Greece, Rome and the Antichrist Empire that is yet to come.

For proof let us look at Revelation 17, beginning at verse nine:

> And here is the mind which hath wisdom. The seven heads are seven mountains, on which the woman [the great spiritual whore] sitteth. And there are seven kings: five are fallen [Egypt, Assyria, Babylon, Medo-Persia, Greece], and one is [the Roman empire which was in power at the time of John's vision], and the other is not yet come; and when he cometh, he must continue a short space [the Antichrist rules for seven years].

From here John goes on to describe the revival of ten nations out of the Old Roman Empire, of which three of these nations will be booted out of the confederacy by the Antichrist, who himself will come from a region where both Rome and Greece extended—boundaries that included parts of Europe and the Middle East. (See Daniel 10:12-21.)

The common thread, however, that is woven throughout the rise of the great empires pointed out by John, is their oppression of Israel. In spite of their glory, they have each been nothing more than Satan's attempt to rule the earth with his "messiah." And following suit, the future Antichrist is coming primarily to take over the temple mount in Jerusalem and rule the world through the Middle East. Satan knows that the world is destined to be ruled from the Middle East—not London or New York, but Israel. Unfortunately, because of their spiritual blindness, the nations of the world are going to cooperate with Satan's policy.

Listen to the words of Zechariah:

> Behold, the day of the Lord is coming, and your spoil will be divided in your midst. For I will gather all the nations to battle against Jerusalem; the city shall be taken, the houses rifled, and the women ravished. Half of the city shall go into captivity, but the remnant of the people shall not be cut off from the city. Then the Lord will go forth and fight against those nations, as He fights in the day of battle. (Zechariah 14:1-3)

And against whom is God going to fight? Those nations that are too proud to believe that God's Word actually applies to them; those nations that think they know better than God what Israel should do and what land they should have; those leaders who are too cowardly to stand for justice in the face of oil embargoes and financial loans—those nations will be the ones to see the hand of God do something contrary to five billion people: "In that day the Lord will defend the inhabitants of Jerusalem; the one who is feeble among them in that day shall be like David, and the house of David shall be like God, like the Angel of the Lord before them" (Zechariah 12:8).

Israel is destined to be rescued from the hands of Gentile oppression, even as she was delivered from the hand of Pharaoh when Moses cried, "...Do not be afraid. Stand still, and see the salvation of the Lord, which He will accomplish for you today. For the Egyptians whom you see today, you shall see again no more forever. The Lord will fight for you, and you shall hold your peace" (Exodus 14:13-14).

Israel is set to be rescued—only this time their exodus will be not only from Egypt but from the four corners of the earth. It will be the final march that will end their 2,500 years of wandering.

Therefore, behold, the days come, saith the Lord, that it shall no more be said, The Lord liveth, that brought up the children of Israel out of the land of Egypt; But, the Lord liveth, that brought up the children of Israel from the land of the north, and from the lands whither he had driven them: and I will bring them again into their land that I gave unto their fathers. (Jeremiah 16:14-15)

Behold, I will bring them from the north country, and gather them from the coasts of the earth, and with them the blind and the lame, the woman with child and her that travaileth with child together: a great company shall return thither. (Jeremiah 31:8)

I will say to the north, Give up; and to the south, Keep not back: bring my sons from far, and my daughters from the ends of the earth. (Isaiah 43:6)

Let the engine of the jets roar, and the pilots prepare for take off. Fill the planes to capacity and clear the runways—the day is coming when every Jew will go home to Israel from the four corners of the earth, and the stigma that has been attached to this people for 2,000 years will suddenly become a divine strength of honor and great respect.

8

The Millennial Throne

We have now arrived at the subject of the Millennium. The millennial reign of Christ—the Kingdom Age—is not a new concept. But because the subject has been left unexplored until now and some reject the idea altogether, I want us to take a moment to lay a solid foundation of proof that such an age is coming.

At least one thousand years before Jesus was born, God announced the fact of His millennial throne through the house of David. Looking at his own beautiful house of cedar one day, David declared it unfair that God should still dwell in a tent. Calling for Nathan the prophet, David expressed his desire to build God a temple. Nathan agreed with David's zeal and they parted company. That same night however, God spoke to Nathan the prophet, saying, "Go tell my servant David, thus saith the Lord, thou shalt not build me an house to dwell in...furthermore I tell you that the Lord will build thee an house" (1 Chronicles 17:3,4,10).

God, not man, shapes history. Anytime we think we have heard from God, we must be open to allow God to alter our first impression. The Church is a wonderful and sacred act of God, but Jesus, not the Church is the Savior of the world. In his best intentions man has always overestimated himself and underestimated God. God reminded both Nathan and David of this. Yet He did it in a most ennobling way. God was about to alter David's good idea, but He had no intention of altering David's righteous zeal for the kingdom of God. Therefore, God began His Word by calling David His "servant." "Thus shalt thou say unto my servant David," He said to Nathan.

In using this particular word, God bestowed upon David a dignity few men have ever received. The word "servant" used by God signifies a prime minister or vicegerent of God, *one who acts in the place of a superior.* David's leadership was clearly a signal to the world that there is an Eternal King to come who will act in the place of God. God not only encouraged David and corrected his good intentions, but He promised David that "His son will build an house...and will establish his kingdom. He shall build me an house, and I will establish his throne forever" (1 Chronicles 17:12). God spoke here of a dual promise to David, that Solomon his son would build a temporary kingdom which no contemporary would be able to rival. God also spoke to David of his future Descendant that would come from his loins through Solomon—Jesus the Messiah. "He will build Me a kingdom, a house and a throne forever" (1 Chronicles 17:14).

One thousand years later, Luke described the birth of that sovereign from David's line saying:

> Now in the sixth month the angel Gabriel was sent by God to a city of Galilee named Nazareth, to a vir-

gin betrothed to a man whose name was Joseph, of the house of David. The virgin's name was Mary....Then the angel said to her, "Do not be afraid, Mary, for you have found favor with God. And behold, you will conceive in your womb and bring forth a Son, and shall call His name Jesus. He will be great, and will be called the son of the Highest; and the Lord God will give unto Him the throne of His father David. And He will reign over the house of Jacob forever, and of His kingdom there will be no end." (Luke 1:26,27,30-33)

The plan was now clear. What God had promised David was coming to pass. His kingdom and his throne would last forever. Through Jesus, a descendant of David through Solomon, Satan and his host of fallen angels were "spoiled"—totally "stripped" of all legal right to govern the earth (See Colossians 2:15.) Jesus then returned to heaven, from which He will come again a second time to establish His eternal throne and continue David's house eternally.

It is almost more than the mind can comprehend. It is almost more than we are willing to believe. But the hard facts contained in this budding revelation of the Millennial kingdom is that one day David's bones that have been entombed for 3,000 years will vibrate the wall of his tomb, and the Divine promise encased in those bones will begin to energize David's body and it will come leaping before the resurrected Savior in the same way he leaped and danced before the ancient Ark of the Covenant. And his family name, his house, will be revived in answer to the prayer he prayed 3,000 years ago!

Do you ever question if God really answers prayer? How long must we wait? The answer is, some prayers will not be answered this side of the Millennium. All prayers will be answered then. Three thousand years ago David prayed.

> Restore us, O God of our salvation, and cause Your anger toward us to cease. Will You be angry with us forever? Will You prolong Your anger to all generations? Will You not revive us again, that Your people may rejoice in You? Show us Your mercy, O Lord, and grant us Your salvation. (Psalm 85:4-7)

David died and was buried. The royal house of David ceased to exist less than five hundred years later. It looked as though David's prayers had fallen on a brass heaven. But in the year A.D. 63, the Holy Spirit moved on a physician named Luke, and he began to describe how God had taken a "break" as it were from Israel, to go into the Gentile world to take a people for Himself: "How God at the first did visit the Gentiles to take out of them a people for His name" (Acts 15:14). This clearly refers to the Church age which is now in progress. However, Luke goes on to say that, "After this I will return, and will build again the tabernacle of David, which is fallen down; and I will build again the ruins thereof, and I will set it up" (verse 16).

David had a plan to build God a house, but God's plan for David was far greater. God would take David's house—his family line—and from it He would bring forth the eternal throne of His Savior. The millennial throne began in David. The confirmations, the parallels between David and Jesus are numerous. Consider the following:

1. David was thirty years old when he began to reign. Samuel records that "David was thirty years old when he began to reign, and he reigned forty years. In Hebron he reigned over Judah seven years and six months, and in Jerusalem he reigned thirty and three years over all Israel and Judah" (2 Samuel 5:4,5).

Jesus was thirty years old when He began to preach the coming kingdom.

2. David did not receive his full kingdom initially. His first army was only a handful of men and women. "His brothers and all his father's house heard it, they went down there to him. And everyone who was in distress, everyone who was it debt, and everyone who was discontented gathered to him. So he became captain over them. And there were about four hundred men with him. (See 2 Samuel 22:1,2)

At his first coming Jesus had only a remnant of followers. His disciples were not the religious Pharisees nor the ruling Sadducees. They were largely the common folk. Mark says, "The common people heard him gladly" (Mark 12:37).

3. David did not receive Jerusalem as his capital for six and one half years. He first ruled from the city of Hebron over two tribes—Judah and Benjamin.

At His first coming, Jesus was rejected by the city of Jerusalem. He wept over it saying, "Jerusalem, Jerusalem, the one who kills the prophets and stones those who are sent to her! How often I wanted to gather your children together as a hen gathers her chicks under her wings, but you were not willing!" (Matthew 23:37). His followers were only a remnant of Israel.

4. David ruled over all Israel for thirty years.

Jesus was crucified at thirty three years. David ruled one year for every year of Messiah's first coming.

5. David desired to build God a permanent house in Jerusalem. "And it came to pass, when David was dwelling in his house, that David said to Nathan the prophet, 'See now, I dwell in a house of cedar, but the ark of the covenant of the Lord is under tent curtains'" (1 Chronicles 17:1). God sent David word, "You shall not build me a house to dwell in" (1 Chronicles 17:4).

Messiah will build the house of God in Jerusalem during the Millennium.

> Behold, the Man whose name is the *branch!* From His place He shall branch out, and He shall build the temple of the Lord; yes, He shall build the temple of the Lord. He shall bear glory, and shall sit and rule on His throne; so He shall be a priest on His throne, and the counsel of peace shall be between them both. (Zechariah 6:12,13)

6. David restored the Word of God to Israel by bringing the ark of the covenant back to Jerusalem. "And it was told King David saying, 'The Lord has blessed the house of Obed-Edom and all that belongs to him, because of the ark of God.' So David went and brought up the ark of God from the house of Obed-Edom to the City of David with gladness. And so it was, when those bearing the ark of the Lord had gone six paces, that he sacrificed oxen and fatted sheep. Then David danced before the Lord with all his might; and David was wearing a linen ephod" (2 Samuel 6:12-15).

The ark represented the Word of God—Jesus. "That which was from the beginning, which we have heard, which we have seen with our eyes, which we have looked upon, and our hands have handled, concerning the Word of life" (1 John 1:1). Just as David brought the ark of God's Word back into Jerusalem with a great processional of praise and worship, *the Word* will descend from heaven with the worship of a great multitude:

> And I heard, as it were, the voice of a great multitude, as the sound of many waters and as the sound of mighty thunderings, saying, "Alleluia! For the Lord God Omnipotent reigns!..." Then I saw heaven opened, and behold, a white horse. And He who sat on him was called Faithful and True...His name is called the Word of God...And He has on His robe and on His thigh a name written: KING OF KINGS AND LORD OF LORDS. (Revelation 19:6,13,16)

7. David conquered his enemies: "Then the fame of David went out into all lands, and the Lord brought the fear of him upon all nations" (1 Chronicles 14:17).

Jesus will conquer all nations. "All the ends of the world shall remember and turn to the Lord, and all the families of the nations shall worship before You" (Psalms 22:27).

8. David ruled with judgment and justice: "So David reigned over all Israel; and David administered judgment and justice to all his people" (2 Samuel 8:15).

Jesus will rule by the same constitution: "For unto us a Child is born, unto us a Son is given; and the government will be upon His shoulder. And His name will be called Wonderful, Counselor, Mighty God, Everlasting Father, Prince of Peace. Of the increase of His government and peace there will be no end, upon the throne of David and over His kingdom, to order it and establish it with judgment and justice from that time forward, even forever..." (Isaiah 9:6,7).

9. David ruled over Israel from Jerusalem.

Jesus will rule from Jerusalem over Israel, as well as all nations. "And He said to me, 'Son of man, this is the place of My throne and the place of the soles of My feet, where I will dwell in the midst of the children of Israel forever. No more shall the house of Israel defile My holy name, they nor their kings...'" (Ezekiel 43:7).

10. David's clothing proclaimed the coming priest-king office of Messiah: "David was clothed with a robe of fine linen, as were all the Levities who bore the ark, the singers, and Chenaniah the music master with the singers. David also wore a linen ephod" (1 Chronicles 15:27). The linen ephod was the garment for priests and Levities alone who served in the temple. Yet David was permitted by God to wear it as a type of the priesthood of Jesus when He rules the earth as Priest-King during the Millennium. The coming government of God is going to be a combination of church and state. Every law will be weighed by the godly standard in the age about to come upon earth.

The parallels between the kingdom of David and the millennial Kingdom of Christ are too numerous to exhaust in this one chapter. Nevertheless, it is evident that David's kingdom was the embryo of the full adult Kingdom of the Lord Jesus that is coming. It is the kingdom age in which Israel and the Church will rule and reign in their various resurrection positions, just as God promised David; "His seed shall endure forever, and his throne as the sun before Me; it shall be established forever like the moon, even like the faithful witness in the sky" (Psalm 89:36,37).

The Kingdom—the Heartbeat of God

The mandate for the "house of David" was to establish on earth what God had decreed from heaven—the foundations for His coming kingdom. David's natural kingdom was a pledge of God's coming kingdom from heaven. The hope of the human race literally rests in "the Root and the offspring of David" (Revelation 22:16).

The hope of worldwide redemption has narrowed down to one Lord, one faith, one baptism. From the broad stream of humanity God selected one man named Abraham. The stream narrowed to one of his sons Isaac. It narrowed again to one of Isaac's sons, Jacob. From Jacob came Judah, from Judah came King David, and through him God fixed the banks of redemption forever. Messiah the Redeemer— the Savior—would sit on David's throne to rule the nations forever. Any hope for saving planet earth is limited to the "house of David."

The Millennium is one of the most relevant subjects today. It will literally affect every person alive at this moment.

What is the Millennium?

When Jesus was put on trail for declaring His Divine and royal commission as King of Israel, Pilate, the Roman governor over Judea asked Him, "Art thou the King of the Jews?" (John 18:33).

Although Jesus never gave Pilate a "Yes" or "No" answer, His response provides us with tremendous information. "My kingdom is not of this world." To understand this statement, we need to know that the Bible reveals two kingdoms—one is universal and the other is time limited. "The Lord has established his throne in heaven, and his kingdom rules over all" (Psalm 103:19). The universal Kingdom of God rules all time, space and creation. It will last forever. The mediatorial or millennial kingdom of Christ is earthwide. It is limited in time to one thousand years. Its purpose is to provide a transitional period between human government and eternity. It is one thousand years of time assigned for the restoration of an earth and a society devastated by sin. This "timed" kingdom exists within the "untimed" universal kingdom. Jesus said clearly that He has a kingdom that is yet to come. Since the universal kingdom of God is always present, Jesus the mediator, could only have been referring to His mediatorial kingdom of one thousand years - the Millennium -which is a phase of the universal kingdom of God.

The Millennium is the New Age that the world unwittingly keeps trying to bring about by throwing off all godly restraint. But Paul wrote of Jesus that "He must reign, until he has put all enemies under his feet" (1 Corinthians 15:25). Without exception, every power in heaven and on earth, from the man in the cave to the most powerful president of a nation will one day be brought into total submission to the authority of the kingdom of heaven. This is the overriding purpose of the period referred to as the Millennium.

9

Will Sin Exist in the Millennium?

The Millennium will not be perfect. It is not heaven, nor the perfection of life lived there in the presence of God. The Millennium will be 1,000 years of moving in the spiritual and moral direction of heaven, under the leadership of Messiah.

Creation began in a sinless state. Man was created with an immortal body, and had he not sinned he would have lived forever in that state. Originally, Adam was not cursed with sin and death; the earth was not cursed with drought, weeds and pollution; and animals were not cursed with a violent nature. The reign of Christ will be for the purpose of restoring the earth to its original curse-free state of life and productivity. "For He must reign till He has put all enemies under His feet" (1 Corinthians 15:25). Paul wrote of this unique period of recovery toward which we are headed.

According to Paul, the power of Christ to do such a restoration is confirmed by "...the exceeding greatness of his power [which is].... Far above all principality, and power, and might, and dominion, and every name that is named, not only in this world, but also in that which is to come (Ephesians 1:19a, 21). "But" as Hebrews states, "Now we see [not yet see] all things put under Him" (Hebrews 2:8).

The work of the Millennium will be to complete the total submission of all creation to Christ and the standard of His Word. For the meek, teachable person, it will be a day of deliverance. For the proud and those resistant to truth, a day of sharp rebuke. Isaiah said, "For the day of the Lord of hosts shall come upon everything proud and lofty, upon everything lifted up—and it shall be brought low—the loftiness of man shall be bowed down, and the haughtiness of men shall be brought low; the Lord alone will be exalted in that day" (Isaiah 2:12,17).

Contrary to our image of Jesus as the Man most qualified to head up the "toddler games" at the Sunday School picnic, Jesus is going to rule the nations with unprecedented authority. His policies will neither be recommendations nor suggestions of heavenly standards, but Jesus is going to enforce absolute divine law and order.

> But with righteousness He shall judge the poor, and reprove with equity for the meek of the earth: and He shall smite the earth: with the rod of His mouth, and with the breath of His lips He shall slay the wicked. And righteousness shall be the girdle of His loins, and faithfulness the girdle of His reins. (Isaiah 11:4-5)

Do you know what that word "smite" means? It comes form the Hebrew *nakah*, and means to give a blow with the hand or fist or a weapon. It means to wound, even to slaughter, or kill.

The human race has never quite gotten the picture: Sin kills. We watch the nightly televised parade of man's approach to sin. Man debates sin's results, but we never take the steps necessary to eradicate the source.

After all, it wouldn't be right! How could we possibly make sin illegal? Who would set the standards? Without a frame of reference, there is no universal way of standardizing right and wrong behavior. It takes a "frame of reference" to have law and order.

Practicing good law has always been complicated by the loophole of changing standards. But practicing law during the Millennium is going to be greatly simplified. By comparison, the legal libraries of the kingdom period are going to be reduced to materials built around one constitution.

There may well be countless volumes of legal documents written during that 1,000 years of litigation in the courts, but they will all be written on the principles of the undisputed divine standard. Moreover, the Supreme Court will be the twenty-four ruling judges who sit around the throne of God in support of His constitution. (See Revelation 4:4.)

Few people realize how legally binding God's Word is. His Word is the power that maintains order throughout the universe. It dictates the paths of the heavenly bodies and orders the steps of all creation.

As Commander in Chief of a nation, Joshua declared that God's Word would be the key to their success as a people. "This Book of the Law shall not depart from your mouth, but you shall meditate in it day and night, that you may observe to do according to all that is written in it. For then you will make your way prosperous, and then you will have good success" (Joshua 1:8).

It may be a surprise to many, but the first Psalm of Messiah's coming reign is addressed partially to the executive and judiciary branches of government. "Be wise now therefore, O ye kings: be instructed, ye judges of the earth" (Psalm 2:10).

In the Millennium, lawyers and judges will be required to meditate on the Law according to Scripture, just as today's priests and ministers meditate and seek its application for living. God's Word has legal application. It is the eternal law by which all things consist and by which men will one day learn to function.

Anyone who knows the Bible will know the basic tenets of the millennial constitution and will have no problem staying out of trouble.

Anyone opposed to God's Word during the Millennium will find himself or herself promptly realigned by it—if he or she wants to stay alive.

"But isn't that rather harsh and dictatorial?" Not when you understand that sin and rebellion produce death. Jesus' chief aim in coming again is to destroy death and every tributary that feeds into its machinery.

The Millennium will be a time when man comes to grips with the harsh realities of sin. There will be sin, sinners and death in the Millennium, but they will not be in the majority. Right now the light of God on the earth is compara-tively weak. His people are not in key places. The voice of truth is not consulted as the foremost authority.

The Word of God is not held in esteem in the courts and institutions of learning. The ratio of unbelievers to believers is two to one. Spiritual darkness is the real world for two-thirds of today's population. For them, sin and death are the only way to live.

A popular radio talk show in Boston devoted one week to a survey regarding sexual behavior at the close of the twentieth century. During the five programs, immorality was discussed as casually as an appointment with the hairdresser. Senior citizens laughed about committing adultery, while younger people boasted of group involvement mixed with all forms of perversions. And both the host as well as the callers discussed immoral behavior as though it were the accepted standard for the majority.

In the Millennium, these numbers will be reversed. Sinners will not be hosting prime time programming. Rebellion will be something few want to talk about, for the obvious retribution it will bring. Imagine the radical changes in television programing when death and dead works are un-popular, and audiences boo sin. (There was a time like this in America only a few short years ago. Sin used to be unpopular.)

The majority of the people of the Millennium are going to be rejoicing, celebrating people who have no interest in sin nor any kind of behavior that promotes death. They will be people hungry to stay alive and prosper with the "sure thing." Isaiah wrote of this day saying:

> ...Be glad and rejoice forever in what I create; for behold, I create Jerusalem as a rejoicing, and her people a joy. No more shall an infant from there live but a few days, nor an old man who has not fulfilled his days; for the child shall die one hundred years old, but the sinner being one hundred years old shall be accursed. (Isaiah 65:18,20)

In other words, a person one hundred years old will be considered a child during the Millennium. No godly person will die prematurely. Only sinners will be subject to early death during that period. Men will live, as Abraham and Methuselah lived, to be hundreds of years old, even the full thousand. Methuselah lived 969 years, Noah 950.

It was only after sin increased that life on earth decreased and God said of man, "his days shall be an hundred and twenty years" (Genesis 6:3). But we find later in Scripture that the years were ultimately reduced to a mere seventy or eighty. Imagine, we went from living 969 years to seventy or less!

Sin has short-changed the whole human race and robbed us of the thing we treasure most—our lives. Sin is death. Sinners promote death. Sex-ridden, immoral films, television shows, pornographic art and books, greed, violence, and human pride lead people by their senses into a miserable flesh-bound existence that brings life to a sudden end.

An expose of a young, successful producer's life was aired one evening. From poverty he had climbed the media ladder, graduating from one of the finest eastern universities only to make his mark early on prime-time television. Suddenly his whole world came to an abrupt halt when he discovered he was dying with AIDS contracted through an immoral lifestyle. His broken-hearted mother just shook her head in grief.

> But know this, that in the last days perilous times will come. For men will be lovers of themselves, lovers of money, boasters, proud, blasphemers, disobedient to parents, unthankful, unholy, unloving, unforgiv-ing, slanderers, without self-control, brutal, despisers of good, traitors, headstrong, haughty, lovers of pleasure rather than lovers of God. (2 Timothy 3:1-4)

This is the kind of world into which Jesus will be coming—a world in desperate need of restoration. And this is where the immortal Church will come so beautifully into position.

Sometime after His arrival, perhaps shortly thereafter, Jesus will gather national representatives to judgment for their mistreatment of Israel. He will determine who deserves death and who should continue to operate as a distinct nation.

> When the Son of Man comes in His glory, and all the holy angels with Him, then He will sit on the throne of His glory. All the nations will be gathered before Him, and He will separate them one from another, as a shepherd divides his sheep from the goats. (Matthew 25:31-32)

The goats refer to the nations who joined the empire of Antichrist to overthrow the statehood of Israel, and the Jewish people. Jesus will be a one-man United Nations whose one vote will seal the fate of all countries.

Following this judgment, the resurrected and raptured saints—the immortals—along with the missionaries from Israel, will be sent out from Jerusalem to preach the gospel among the nations. We will rule and reign as "kings" in various positions of leadership for the purpose of purifying every human institution in existence. The earth will not be converted into full-blown righteousness overnight. Isaiah said of Messiah's kingdom "Of the increase of His government and peace, there will be no end..." (Isaiah 9:7).

The government of Messiah Jesus will "increase" across the earth, as the Church has spread for the past 2,000 years. From 120 Jewish believers in an upper room, we have become billions upon billions of redeemed people. Even so, the Millennium will be a time of heaven's increase on the earth.

How quickly we will spread, how quickly our message will be received, we do not know. But this one thing is certain, we will do it in the power of the same Spirit by which we now operate. "The zeal of the Lord of hosts will perform it," said Isaiah.

Do you know what the word "zeal" implies? It means that the saints of God will be dispatched across this earth in "a state of passionate commitment." Zeal means "passionate commitment." The kingdom of Messiah will spread, not with lame intimidation and half-hearted ef-fort, but with passionate commitment we will blaze the trail from country to country and island to island, until every tribe, tongue and people at every level of society hears that the King reigns in Jerusalem! And His ways bring eternal life!

As a result of the spreading of this "good news," which the world has always misunderstood, there will be the healing of the nations for which we have always longed. Isaiah wrote of the millennial people that, "They shall not build, and another inhabit; they shall not plant and another eat; for as the days of a tree, so shall be the days of My people, and My elect shall long enjoy the work of their hands" (Isaiah 65:22).

People of the Millennium will be like well-watered trees. The works of the godly will not wither halfway through their project, but whatever they do will prosper to its maximum potential. Business failures will be unheard of among God's people. Lost opportunities and dying careers will no longer plague the faithful. Hard work will bear its fruit in due season.

Trees live hundreds, even thousands of years. The 5,000- years-old Bristlecone Pines and the Baobab Trees of Africa are the oldest living things. In today's society "things" often outlive their inventors and creators, but the time is coming when people will be the oldest living things on earth.

As rebellion is being put down by the teaching of God's Word, and men begin to see that the knowledge of God extends life indefinitely, they will become radical to learn more of Him. Bible study is certain to become epidemic. Prayer meetings will spread like wildfire.

Yes, millennial people will enjoy prayer on a level largely unknown today. Isaiah said we will get answers before we even ask. "And it shall come to pass, that before they call, I will answer; and while they are yet speaking, I will hear" (Isaiah 65:24). This will be possible of course, because Satan will be bound.

Imagine a prayer where the answer comes before you can get the words out of your mouth. In the middle of the sentence—there it will be. Men will be praying from morning till night. They will wake up praising God and making their requests known to Him. It will literally be the fulfilling of the promise that "nothing will be impossible to him that believes."

What couldn't you accomplish if you could wake up tomorrow morning and say, "Lord, what should I do with this person? This company? This proposal?" And while you are yet trying to figure out the direction to take, the Spirit of God very clearly says, "This is what you should do...." (In fact, there is no reason we should not be walking in this realm already. God is the same today, as He will be in the Millennium.)

Prayer is a fountainhead for continual miracles. It works today, it will only increase for the millennial prayer war-rior. Intercession should be one of the most desirable posi-tions in the Church. It is like "magic" fountains flowing with the demonstrations of God.

Imagine the frustration of the sinners in the Millennium when godly people, realizing the power of prayer, always beat them to the best positions because God heard their prayers and told them how to take hold of the opportunity.

But would God actually promote His people above the doubtful? No question, He promises that if we humble ourselves He will exalt us in due season.

Jesus' Prayers

Jesus never prayed as man prays. He had no "Christmas list" nor "mourning parchment." Jesus conversed with God as two adults communicate. Jesus was not begging, grabbing at straws, nor babbling empty words of repetition. He prayed at the resurrection of Lazarus,

> Father, I thank You that You have heard Me And I know that you always hear Me, but because of the people who are standing by I said this, that they may believe that You sent Me. Now when He had said these things, He cried with a loud voice, "Lazarus come forth!" And he who had died came out bound hand and foot with grave clothes, and his face was wrapped with a cloth. Jesus said to them, "Loose him, and let him go." (John 11:41b-44)

That is praying—millennial praying—that will take charge of sin and death and commit it back to hell where it originated.

Prayer is calling on God to exert His supernatural influence on the situation. The reason for persisting in prayer today is not because God is unwilling or unable to respond, rather it is because of Satan's interferences. Prayer today is like calling for help when the people around you are trying to stop your call. You may have to fight vigorously past the interferences in order to be heard, but if you persist with that name that has all authority in the spirit realm, you are bound to get through to heaven's courts. Once you are there, God will exert His supernatural influence on your circumstances and things will happen.

Answer to prayer is the manifestation of God's glory. Jesus' first miracle of turning water into wine was called a manifestation of God's glory. Glory means the manifested presence of God. When the presence of God is made known to us, the glory of God is present.

Thirty-five hundred years ago God vowed by His own life that sin would be put down on the earth, and His glory would be established in its place. Five times in Scripture God has declared it, "...As truly as I live, all the earth shall be filled with the glory of the Lord" (Numbers 14:21).

In Habakkuk He said, "For the earth will be filled with the knowledge of the glory of the Lord, as the waters cover the sea" (Habakkuk 2:14).

Habakkuk goes on to say that God's glory "covered the heavens and the earth was full of His praise," as He led Israel out of Egypt. How much more so will His glory fill the whole earth as the knowledge of Him increases through His millennial prayer warriors.

In her book *Glory*, Ruth Ward Heflin has written, "Earth has the atmosphere of air whereas the heavenly atmosphere is glory." (Ruth Ward Heflin. *Glory*. Shippensburg, PA: Destiny Image, 1990, p. 125.)

One of the great works of the Church during the coming kingdom period will be to destroy sin by spreading the knowledge of God, through inviting demonstrations of His glory, as Jesus invited at Lazarus' tomb.

How much do you recognize the glory of God now? Do you sense His presence often? God is here. But because we slumber in carnality, we often fail to recognize Him. Jesus said where two or three are gathered in His name, He is in their midst. Have you ever seen a vision of Jesus? Felt His breath? Had His hand touch your head? Sensed His embrace? Just felt a little breeze as He walked by? Maybe heard Him speak?

We could, if we knew how to turn off our natural "thought processes" and open our spiritual eyes and ears, if we had the key to "knowing the glory." Knowledge is essential to recognizing the glory.

Is it possible that the knowledge of the glory of God—the manifested presence of God—is not experienced more in the Church because the Church has not been taught to recognize and respect it? How many of us have ever been taught to expect it! By and large, the God we have worshiped has been out of reach.

For the average believer, it is much easier to believe that sinners will be present in a worship service than the presence of God—that more people will leave the service unsaved, unhealed, and unhelped, than set free by the manifested glory of God.

In the Millennium, this will be reversed. Sinners in meetings will be rare. God's manifested, awe-inspiring, miracle-working presence will meet them at the door, and consume them before they can even be seated.

In fact, this should be true today.

10

The Unbroken Good Work

Because this present life looms so big in the minds of men, we have a hard time seeing the continuity between time and eternity. Physical death for most people means extinction of all things that are familiar. The earth, people, relationships, our own personal identity—the things we treasure most in this life we cannot envision existing after physical death.

Even those of us who believe in God generally anticipate a strange, unfamiliar journey awaiting our departure from this present existence. It has never occurred to us that heaven may feel just right when we arrive there, and we may fit into that climate as naturally as we fit in here.

Heaven, however, is not man's final destination—earth is. "The meek shall inherit the earth," Jesus said. But heaven certainly fits into God's plan for our continued development, as surely as going away to a university fits in with all we were before and hope to be thereafter.

In fact, Paul confirmed this very idea when he wrote under the inspiration of the Holy Spirit, "For I am confident of this very thing, that He who has begun a good work in you will perfect it until the day of Jesus Christ" (Philippians 1:6, New American Standard).

The Amplified Bible makes the point even more clearly,

> I am convinced and sure of this very thing, that He who began a good work in you will continue until the day of Jesus Christ—right up to the time of His return—developing [that good work] and perfecting and bringing it to full completion in you... so that you may surely learn to sense what is vital, and approve and prize what is excellent and of real value—recognizing the highest and the best, and distinguishing the moral differences.... (Philippians 1:6-10)

From the moment a person is born of the Spirit, a "good work" begins in his or her life. It is a work designed to train us for "eternal" living, by teaching us what is of real value in life. Since so many people are concerned about the endtime chaos described by the prophets, the Church is inclined to forget that at no time does God ever lose control of things. Man will lose control, but not God. He will continue His "good work" even in the worst of times. Moreover, if God is going to continue developing, maturing, teaching and training His people until Jesus returns, then we can rest assured that good things will continue to happen in the lives of God's people.

We need to remember that whatever God begins is not subject to the changes taking place among men and nations. "For God hath not appointed us to wrath but to obtain salvation through our Lord Jesus Christ" (1 Thessalonians 5:9), Paul reminds us.

Last-days tribulation will be beyond man's control. Catastrophic events will occur between nations, in nature, and in the unseen realm of the spirit. But God's good work will continue right on schedule. What a truth to grasp for the days ahead! What a certainty to remember. How many Christians today live on the verge of panic because they have forgotten that God's good work in their life is still in force regardless of the trials they may be going through.

The Bubonic Plague

In 1348, the Bubonic plague entered Europe from the Near East. Many people considered it to be the judgment of God. And because they forgot that God was still in control, nations turned on each other with a warring hatred. Men were dying all over the world, and those who weren't dying were accusing and killing each other by the thousands.

The plague began in India. And within one year forty-eight million had died.

When the King of Taurus saw his people dying of something that had not touched Christians, he headed for Rome to become a Christian. On his way he learned that the plague had also struck the Christians, so he turned back toward home. The Christians, however, came down upon him and his band and killed about 7,000 of them.

By this time the plague was widespread in England. The Scots suspecting this to be God's judgment on them, took this opportunity to invade England. But the avenging plague had by now struck the Scots. As they prepared to return home, having lost 5,000 of their men to the pestilence, the English pursued and killed a great many more.

Always remembering that God is in charge and doing a good work, regardless of the circumstances, is more than mental satisfaction. It means the difference between life and death. Instead of turning to God in repentance [which some surely did] during the black death, nations turned to each other and, finding no solution, they turned on each other and ended up in senseless battles and more deaths. Desperate men do desperate things. Unless we remember God, we are all capable of becoming lawless.

The Psalmist said, "The wicked shall be turned into hell, and all nations that forget God" (Psalm 9:17). Plagues are destined to mark the closing days of human history, but the greatest plague of all will be "forgetfulness." Men will almost totally forget God, forget that He is in control. Instead of turning toward their solution, John said powerful leaders, intellectuals from every field of study, entrepreneurs, prosperous men, free men in the last days will run from God.

> And the kings of the earth, the great men, the rich men, the commanders, the mighty men, every slave and every free man, hid themselves in the caves and in the rocks of the mountains, and said to the mountains and rocks, "Fall on us and hide us from the face of Him who sits on the throne and from the wrath of the Lamb! For the great day of His wrath has come, and who is able to stand? (Revelation 6:15,16,17)

The truth is, man has an invitation into the presence of God. Any person who remembers God can stand in His strength and see the salvation of God in the midst of great turmoil.

"For we do not have a High Priest who cannot sympathize with our weaknesses, but was in all points tempted as we are, yet without sin. Let us therefore come boldly before the throne of grace, that we may obtain mercy and find grace in time of need" (Hebrews 4:15-16). This is the eternal promise of God. It is a promise that applies as much to the tribulation period as to times of peace.

What God began with Moses and Israel in Egypt, He is perfecting through Jesus' blood-bought disciples. The protecting cloud has not disappeared, nor has the "pillar of fire" gone out. Paul says it will continue until the return of Jesus.

David Stern translates Paul's words this way: "I am sure of this: that the One who began a good work among you will keep it growing until it is completed on the Day of the Messiah, Yeshua.

The work of God is not designed simply to maintain human survival. Hanging on with a handful of beaten down Christians and Jews is not God's idea of a "good work." God's work is destined to keep growing and advancing from now on!

Eternal Word—Eternal Work

Once the commission to write a book on the Millennium became clear to me, I went around for weeks praying this prayer: "Father, show me in Scripture what the Millennium will be like. I want to see it in Scripture." Then one day as I was busy with other things, these words appeared: "All the teachings of Scripture are an explanation of what man can expect during the Millennium. Everything written about 'righteous living' will be the standard policies for the Millennial Kingdom era."

Suddenly, I understood that the Word of God literally is forever. Yes, the Bible contains history, prophecies, poetry, and personal statements about present situations, such as the Apostle Paul's request in one of his letters that his coat be brought to him before winter. But the order of worship, the social, moral, and political policies of God's system of government have never been received by the masses. Compared to the world population since time began, very few people have complied with God's policies one hundred percent.

In the Millennium, however, the majority of men, women, and children will be enrolled in classes of godly policy making. The knowledge of God will continue to be taught just as it is being taught today. Yes, there will be churches during the Millennium. There will be pastors, teachers, and regular worship with sermons. The sermons, of course, will be looking back to the Second Coming, just as Christians look back to the Cross. But natural man will continue to be instructed in the Word in a way that applies to every area of life.

This is the progression: The Jews taught God from the vantage point of the Messiah to come. The Church teaches God, from the vantage point of the Messiah, has come. In the Millennium we will provide all the information as to how it all happened and what it means from here on out.

The Bible will be no more obsolete during the Millennium than the Old Testament is now. The Old Testament was Part One, the New Testament is Part Two, the Millennium will be Part Three.

We will need to study the Bible during the Millennium just as much as we study it now. It contains the story of redemption, the history of Creation, the nature of God, and rules for righteous living and civil justice.

Do we think for one moment that because Jesus is ruling in Jerusalem, we can ignore the Bible and worship services that honor Him and instruct us in His ways? Is He going to have men ushered into a private audience with Him in Jerusalem who have made no effort to learn anything about Him otherwise? I doubt it. Worshipers will be welcomed to the Temple of Messiah, not tourists and "favor seekers." Israel will, though, be deluged with tourists following Armageddon and the defeat of Gog's army.

Ezekiel said,

> It will come to pass in that day that I will give Gog a burial place there in Israel, the valley of those who pass by east of the sea; and it will obstruct travelers, because there they will bury Gog and all his multitude. Therefore they will call it the Valley of Hamon Gog. For seven months the house of Israel will be burying them, in order to cleanse the land. Indeed all the people of the land will be burying them, and they will gain renown for it on the day that I am glorified, says the Lord God.
>
> They will set apart men regularly employed, with the help of a search party, to pass through the land and bury those bodies remaining on the ground, in order to cleanse it. At the end of seven months they will make a search. The search party will pass through land; and whenever anyone sees a man's bone, he shall set up a marker by it, till the buriers have buried it in the Valley of Hamon Gog. (Ezekiel 39:11-15)

"Hamon-Gog" will be on every person's itinerary to Israel. People will be eager to see the valley where Jesus defeated that world-class, overnight political sensation, who strutted before the cameras of the world and bragged about his conquests of Israel and surrounding nations. He who sent out the dreaded code "666" and demanded all the Middle East take it or be eliminated from commercial survival among the nations. "And he causes all, both small and great, rich and poor, free and slave, to receive a mark on their right hand or on their foreheads, and that no one may buy or sell except one who has the mark or the name of the beast, or the number of his name" (Revelation 13:16-17).

He who thought to sit on the holy mountain "in place of Christ"—the Antichrist!—this man and his defeated army will be a major attraction for those who want to see, first-hand, the power of the new King.

Without question, every Israeli tour guide will have his Bible—Old and New Testament in his hands as he points to the same key Scriptures we are now reading. They will read Ezekiel's amazing description of the final war, written approximately 600 B.C., and they will marvel at his accuracy, just as we marvel at Isaiah's accuracy in describing Messiah's birth, death and coming again. Think how exciting it is going to be to look into Scripture in light of the blaring evidence of a massive tomb in Meggido right before our eyes. It will be a time when the truth of the Word will become as obvious as its power. It will be a time when men will come from all parts of the world to examine God's Word in the light of the new King of kings, and the landmarks of His victories.

Another Pentecost

For too long believers have imagined the Second Coming of Jesus as the end when, in fact, there is going to be another great outpouring of the Holy Spirit at His return. "...I will pour upon the house of David, and on the inhabitants of Jerusalem the Spirit of grace..." (Zechariah 12:10), declares God.

Another Pentecost? Yes, it is all a part of the "Latter Rains" that are going to fall upon the earth for a great spread of the gospel for a thousand years.

Israel—God's Pitcher

God has always poured out His Spirit first into the pitcher of Israel. "This people have I formed from myself," he declared. "They shall shew forth my praise." It is from the silver pitcher of Israel that the Spirit has and will continue to pour out His apples of gold upon the earth. Isaiah said,

> Now it shall come to pass in the latter days that the mountain of the Lord's house shall be established on the top of the mountains, and shall be exalted above the hills; and all nations shall flow to it. Many people shall come and say, "Come and let us go up to the mountain of the Lord, to the house of the God of Jacob; He will teach us His ways, and we shall walk in His paths." For out of Zion shall go forth the law, and the word of the Lord from Jerusalem. (Isaiah 2:2-3)

This is speaking of the Millennium. Both the law and the Word will flow from the consecrated land of Israel, and it will spread among the nations for a total restoration. Teaching and correction will still be in order during the Millennium. The minds of men will still need renewing according to truth. Isaiah said of Jesus' reign, "He shall judge among the nations, and shall rebuke many people; and they shall beat their swords into plowshares, and their spears into pruning hooks; nation shall not lift up sword against nation, neither shall they learn war any more" (Isaiah 2:4).

129

Nations will not "learn war," but they will learn. And what they will learn is the Word of God for proper kingdom living. Any politician hoping to get to Israel to meet the new King and gain unjust favors for his country, will be in for a swift course in royal policy.

Jesus will have no problem rebuking the selfish ambitions of the unrenewed or ungodly ruler. Since He looks at all men as equal, no bribes will be taken, no flattering words will influence His judgment, no positions of power will impress nor intimidate Him. His constitution will be fair and clear, but in no way open for human interpretation. The government of the Millennium will be an absolute theocracy. The Constitution will be, in essence, the Ten Commandments. God's Word will be not only final, but nations will be made to understand that His Word is the absolute law written into the code of every gene and atom of creation.

When Isaiah revealed that God's Law will go out from Jerusalem, he did not mean that a series of new concepts are going to be stuffed into numerous oversized legal documents, that would take a Harvard degree to decipher. The law that would go out of Jerusalem during the Millennium will be the restoration of the ancient edict etched by the finger of God into common stone:

1. You shall have no other gods before me.
2. You shall not make unto you any graven images.
3. You shall not take the name of the Lord your God in vain.
4. Remember the Sabbath day to keep it holy.
5. Honor your father and mother.
6. You shall not kill.
7. You shall not commit adultery.

8. You shall not steal.
9. You shall not bear false witness.
10. You shall not covet...anything that is your neighbor's.

The good work of God began the day He spoke the world into existence. It is a work that is eternally linked to man from covenant to covenant by His Word. It is a work from immortality through time and back again into eternity—that one good work that not even Satan with all his legions was able to stop. And it is a work that will delight the eyes of eternity forever—heaven and earth married.

11

Prosperity Is Coming

"In that day I will make a covenant. . .with the beasts of the field, with the birds of the air, and with the creeping things of the ground."

Solomon understood the way the mind of fallen man operates when he said: "The poor man is hated even by his own neighbor, but the rich has many friends" (Proverbs 14:20). We are not impressed with poverty. While many are moved to help the poor, the people who impress us, get our attention, influence our lives are those who have risen above their lack. Overcomers make the news and receive the appointments to positions of power.

Although it can be misleading, prosperity gets our respect. No one seeks the advice of a beggar. A hungry man hardly asks a starving person how to get food. Presently, the wealth of the world is largely in the hands of the ungodly. This makes society under the control of the system of sin. In the Millennium, however, this system will be reversed. There is coming a time of transformation on the earth when everything that lives will prosper as God originally designed. The "meek" not the "chic" are destined to take possession of the world systems, properties, and positions of power.

There is a verse of Scripture that has confused the Church for years. In Revelation 13:7, John says the Antichrist shall make war on the saints and "overcome" them. It is confusing because we know that both Christians and Israel are called to stand their ground, and never bow to Satan's forces. After all, "Greater is he who is in us than he who is in the world." How, then, can an evil power be allowed to prevail?

The answer is that he will not prevail—in the long run. Daniel the prophet wrote of this time, "I was watching; and the same horn was making war against the saints, and prevailing against them, until the Ancient of Days came, and a judgment was made in favor of the saints of the Most High, and the time came for the saints to possess the kingdom" (Daniel 7:21,22).

Antichrist prevails until—his time has run out. In the same way, all evil powers are destined to fail. With the reign of Christ, everything in creation is going to be released from the curse that presently hinders its full expression, and everything that God called "very good" will be good.

In this chapter, we are going to look at some of the interesting changes that are going to come on the earth during the uninterrupted *mille annus* prosperity. You will be shocked to learn just how many things are now being held back because of the curse of sin, and you will be excited to learn about all the dramatic changes that will accompany sin's eviction.

At the outset, it will help us to acknowledge the fact that God has marked off this period of 1,000 years as unique from all other periods of time. Jesus was ruling with God before He came to earth in flesh. He has been ruling at His right hand ever since. In fact, only 33 years of time have occurred when Christ was not ruling the heavens and the earth. Those are the years when He humbled Himself to take a fleshly body and die for man's salvation. With the exception of Christ's incarnate thirty-three years among man, however, He has been the divine sovereign ruling from the heavens for eons.

Then why has God called attention to a particular 1,000 years time frame? What makes this time period so special? The answer is because this particular time has been set aside for the recovery of something dear to God.

Genesis records that at creation, "God saw everything that He had made, and behold, it was very good..." (Genesis 1:31).

Everything God created was made to fulfill a good purpose. God didn't create something and then decide a use for it. He first saw the need and then He designed an instrument to fit that purpose.

The ultimate purpose of all things in creation is to express some form of God's glory. Heavenly lights, plants, animals, water, air—everything that has life—reflects some degree of God's glory.

To some extent, Adam and Eve experienced that fuller glory in creation. For example, they enjoyed a relationship with animals that we know nothing about.

Scientists sit in caves, deserts, tents, and trees for years trying to discover the life patterns of animals, birds, and insects. We are fascinated by the habits of the beautiful creatures around us. That honey bees can signal the location of food when it is somewhere else amazes us.

"Fellows, there is a large load of crumbs to the left of the old barn," the queen calls out to her workers. What a puzzle this is to science, but Adam had no such barrier. He called the animals to himself and communicated on a level of exchange that was perfectly normal—otherwise the serpent would not have been able to talk with Eve.

Do you realize that Eve was not the least surprised when the serpent initiated a conversation with her? Even on spiritual matters!

So far as we have record, that the serpent should mention God seemed no surprise at all to Adam or Eve. Its manner was so ordinary that it was able to make its point quite successfully. A deceived, talking serpent helped to bring about the downfall of the entire human race. Yes, a reptile with an intellect far superior to any reptilian brain power we know today was deceived into cooperating with Satan. This is also how the animal kingdom came under the curse, and all animals became wild and unable to communicate with man or each other. This is how death—the survival of the fittest—became the nature of the animal world, and grieved God.

Yes, God is grieved at the curse that has turned His gentle, trusting, beautiful animal world into a band of vicious, blood-thirsty, scared killers.

Do you recall Job's famous encounter with God? Are you aware that most of the questions God posed to Job were about the animal kingdom?

> Can you hunt the prey for the lion, or satisfy the appetite of the young lions, when they crouch in their dens, or lurk in their lairs to lie in wait? Who provides food for the raven, when its young ones cry to God,

and wander about for lack of food? Do you know the time when the wild mountain goats bear young?... Or can you mark when the deer gives birth? The wings of the ostrich wave proudly, but are her wings and pinions like the kindly stork's? For she leaves her eggs on the ground, and warms them in the dust. Have you given the horse strength? Have you clothed his neck with thunder?... Does the hawk fly by your wisdom, and spread its wings toward the south? Does the eagle mount up at your command, and make its nest on high? Look now at the behemoth, which I made along with you; he eats grass like an ox. His bones are like beams of bronze, his ribs like bars of iron. Who has preceded Me, that I should pay him? Everything under heaven is Mine (Job 38:39-41;39:1,13-14, 19,26,27;40:15,18; 41:11).

The animal kingdom is something dear to God. It is one part of creation that is presently suffering from the curse of man's rebellion. It is in fact "in labor."

Paul wrote concerning this:

For the earnest expectation of the creation eagerly waits for the revealing of the sons of God. For the creation was subjected to futility, not willingly, but because of Him who subjected it in hope; because the creation itself also will be delivered from the bondage of corruption into the glorious liberty of the children of God. For we know that the whole creation groans and labors with birth pangs together until now. (Romans 8:19-22)

The animal kingdom groans and is in misery because of the curse of death upon it. Any hunter will tell you that to kill an animal you have to sit without making one single sound in order to get close enough to shoot. They are running scared. The breaking of one small twig is enough to send an animal leaping immediately out of sight. Try stepping on an insignificant insect and watch how it runs for cover. Survival is a natural instinct in everything that lives. But communication among the species so that the threat is removed is impossible. People may stop wearing furs, but who will tell bears not to kill people or other animals?

Human beings are incapable of eradicating death. And so long as there is death, aggression will drive creation to attack itself.

The prophecy of Isaiah says: "The wolf also shall dwell with the lamb, the leopard shall lie down with the young goat, the calf and the young lion and the fatling together; and a little child shall lead them" (Isaiah 11:6).

This does not mean that wild animals in the Millennium will only become domesticated, but there will be a divine transformation in the very nature of animals. We know this because of the statement that follows next: "The cow and the bear shall graze; their young ones shall lie down together; and the lion shall eat straw like the ox" (Isaiah 11:7).

All animals that now kill for meat will change to eating vegetation in the new kingdom. This radical change will occur because animals will no longer have the killing nature. The original nature with which God created them, a nature with which man can communicate, will be restored.

In speaking to Job, God describes how He has presently limited the brain power of the animal world. Of the ostrich He says that she,

...leaves her eggs on the ground, and warms then in the dust; she forgets that a foot may crush them, or that a wild beast may break them. She treats her young harshly, as though they were not hers; her labor is in vain, without concern, because God deprived her of wisdom, and did not endow her with understanding. (Job 39:14-17)

Do you mean God is going to communicate on a greater level with His creatures? Why not? He has already spoken through a donkey to the erring prophet Balaam. He spoke to a group of ravens to feed His faithful prophet Elijah. He spoke to a whale to regurgitate Jonah out of its stomach. He spoke to the deceived serpent that passed on its deception to Eve, telling the serpent that it would crawl on its stomach forever. And God will call great numbers of birds to the valley of Armageddon for the Marriage Supper of the Lamb.

Yes, God communicates with all His creatures and commissions them for blessing or curse. In the Millennium, earthly creatures will return to their original level of communication with God, with man and with each other. It will doubtless be a time when their usefulness will become far more obvious than it is now. Carrier pigeons, beasts of burden, plow horses, milk-producing cows and goats, and watch dogs are just a hint of the prosperity that is coming through the creature kingdom.

God speaking through Ezekiel said, "I will multiply upon you man and beast; and they shall increase and bring fruit" (Ezekiel 36:11). Who knows what an animal set free from the curse is capable of performing?

Perhaps animals also use only fifteen percent of their brain power. It may be that a farmer in the Millennium will be plowing a field when his horse will turn around and say,

"Nitrogen is low in this field," or "It will rain tomorrow—I can feel it in my hoofs."

"Fear not, O land; be glad and rejoice: for the Lord will do great things," writes Joel. "Be not afraid, ye beasts of the field: for the pastures of the wilderness do spring, for the tree beareth her fruit, the fig tree and the vine do yield their strength" (Joel 2:22).

Creation is in labor. It groans as a quadriplegic groans—with trapped abilities, and lifeless unfulfilled plans and desires. We know there is more, but the strength to make it work is just not there. The average person runs out of life long before he runs out of dreams and desires. Age comes swiftly into our physical houses and causes us to slow down at a time when we are just getting the "hang" of things. Sin has stripped creation of its full strength and beauty.

Do you know that a time is coming when light from the planets will be increased sevenfold? Isaiah said, "...The light of the moon shall be as the light of the sun, and the light of the sun shall be sevenfold, as the light of seven days, in the day that the Lord bindeth up the breach of his people, and healeth the stroke of their wound" (Isaiah 30:26).

Imagine a world where the heavens become illuminated with seven times their present light. What will the stars look like when they sparkle seven times brighter? What kind of growth will take place on earth when the sun shines down with seven times more life-giving rays? Germination will accelerate at such a rate, we will be able to plant and harvest in the same month.

What will this earth be like under God's coming restoration of man, beasts, and the celestial bodies? What will God's new kingdom "lighting system" bring about?

12

The Desert Will Blossom

Although the West Coast of the United States of America has a limited desert region, by and large we are a fertile, green country. Not until the year 1990 did we begin to think about the reality of living in a land of desert. This happened because tens of thousands of young American, British, and European servicemen and women went to a little known spot in the Middle East to help resolve a conflict between two countries.

I wish to acknowledge an article from *Zion's Fire* called "Babylon the Eclipse of Eden," written by Pastor Dan Hayden as one source of information for the opening of this chapter.

To most westerners it was simply "another Middle East feud." But in the realm of the spirit, what happened in 1990 was a turning of history toward its final approach to the millennial runway and the beginning of God's kingdom rule on earth.

Stop and think about it—the minds of the whole world suddenly dropped everything else of importance, and people everywhere looked toward the one spot on earth where God came down thousands of years ago and planted a beautiful garden to cradle His newborn man. It was a cradle that would cast a shadow all the way to our generation, with the threat of war.

After a few weeks of fighting in the Middle East, however, the world found itself ready to pull out, applaud a quick victory, and go on. But like Brier Rabbit's "tar-baby", the eyes of the world can expect to return again and again to this spot in the future. What we shall be seeing will be a painful turning of the soil for the restructuring of the desert and a time of restoration.

At Disney's famous Epcot Center there is an interesting exhibit where they demonstrate how primeval rain forests created the underground reservoirs of energy resources we have today. Through pressure and time, decay produces energy resources such as coal and oil. Using this premise, is it not feasible that during the Flood, the Garden of Eden with its lush, uncursed vegetation was turned upside down and buried deep within the earth, and ultimately became the abundant oil supply beneath the Middle Eastern floor of Iraq and Kuwait?

According to popular consensus, the Garden of Eden lay somewhere in the region of Mesopotamia. Two of the four rivers mentioned in the Garden (Genesis 2:11-14) are definitely identifiable: the Tigris and the Euphrates, located in the region of southern Iraq and Kuwait.

The reason for the divine "plowing under" of the garden, as we know, was sin. What we have not grasped is the fact that Babylon, as the womb of evil in the world and the birthplace of every false religion, casts a long shadow across the entire face of civilization. John called her "the mother of harlots and abominations of the earth" (Revelation 17:5).

This means that the region of Iraq has been, is, and will continue to be the object of divine judgment, as the world makes its final approach to the millennial runway.

Zechariah's Vision

Around 550 B.C. when Israel had returned from exile in Babylon, a prophet named Zechariah had a series of visions from the Lord. One of these visions is particularly interesting in regard to Babylon and its continued career of evil. Zechariah writes:

> Then the angel who talked with me came out and said to me, "lift your eyes now, and see what this is that goes forth." So I asked, "What is it?" And he said, "It is a basket that is going forth." He also said, "This is their resemblance throughout the earth: Here is a lead disc lifted up, and this is a woman sitting inside the basket;" then he said, "This is Wickedness!"
>
> And he thrust her down into the basket, and threw the lead cover over its mouth. Then I raised my eyes and looked, and there were two women, coming with the wind in their wings; for they had wings like the wings of a stork, and they lifted up the basket between earth and heaven. So I said to the angel who talked with me, "Where are they carrying the basket?" And he said to me, "To build a house for it in the land of Shinar; when it is ready, the basket will be set there on its base." (Zechariah 5:5-11)

What Zechariah saw was actually wickedness in the form of a woman being transported in a basket to the land of Shinar—Babylon. There the woman (wickedness) would have a house of worship built for her. Even though there was a heavy lid on the basket weighing "a talent of lead"— 122 pounds—nothing would be able to hold wickedness down. In the last days, the lid of wickedness will be lifted— commerce, false religion, and political chaos will be unleashed from the region of Babylonia-Iraq, and the whole world will feel the effects of it.

A Brief History of Iraq

Historically, if we go back to such names as Sumeria, Shinar, Babylonia, and Assyria, we will find ourselves referring to the region known today as Iraq. Iraq actually became an independent state as recently as 1927, when Britain, as mandatory of the area, granted statehood to the region under the throne of King Emir Faisal. They became an official member of the League of Nations in 1932, and gained their total freedom in 1947, at the end of World War II.

The womb of evil was now getting ready to initiate its final approach. Babylon had "thrown its hat" into the twentieth century political arena, and its intentions were made known by the very next year. On May 14, 1948, Iraq, along with Transjordan, invaded the new state of Israel.

Four thousand years ago in Ur of Sumaria, God said to a man named Abram:

> ...Get thee out of thy country, and from thy kindred, and from thy father's house, unto a land that I will shew thee: And I will make of thee a great nation, and I will bless thee, and make thy name great; and thou shalt be a blessing: And I will bless them that bless thee, and curse him that curseth thee: and in thee shall all families of the earth be blessed. (Genesis 12:1-3)

Babylonia was cursed. Sin had entered the human race there. After the Flood, Noah's grandson's, Cush and Nimrod, had revived the religious heresy of their ancestors. Next door in Persia were the descendants of rebellious Cain, who first introduced murder into the world. And 2,500 years later, to the south in Saudi Arabia, would come the birth of Islam through Mohammed. Satan's headquarters was firmly established in and surrounding the Babylonian region.

God's headquarters would never be in that area. Therefore, Abraham was called to journey approximately 700 miles west of Iraq to the land of Canaan. It was here that God would establish His covenant with the land and the people for the coming millennial reign of His Son, Jesus.

Abraham was a Babylonian. So were the wives of his son and grandson, Isaac and Jacob. But once the call to "come out" of Babylon was sent forth, Abraham and his descendants stood forever in direct contrast to everything Babylon represented. It was a contrast with irreconcilable differences that would only increase with time. It was and is a difference that will one day explode into Armageddon and the end of the age-old contest between God and Satan.

Babylon will be a key player in the days ahead. Satan's career began there. But it will end on God's home turf in Israel. It is from there the deserts of the Middle East will be set free from their curse, and they will recover their ability to blossom as the rose. It is one of the great acts of restoration that is going to take place under the reign of Messiah. The only question remaining is, how will He accomplish it?

Contrary to what we might assume with our knowledge of the region, God does not say oil will be the key to

His act of restoring the deserts of the Middle East, or any desert region in the world. Water, not oil, is the key to life on planet earth. Growing up on a farm, I learned early the value of water. No water; no food.

A large part of the Middle East depends on the Euphrates River for its water supply. The Euphrates originates in Turkey, flows through Syria and Iraq, joins the Tigris and flows all the way down to the Persian Gulf.

In 1990, Turkey completed its new Ataturk Dam. In order to fill the dam, it capped off the flow of the Euphrates, and so frightened Syria and Iraq that they threatened war if the flow did not resume. Some projections are that once the southeast Anatolia project of twenty-one dams and seventeen hydroelectric power plants is finished, Turkey will control both the Tigris and the Euphrates Rivers. How easy it would then be to fulfill John's word in Revelation 16:12: "Then the sixth angel poured out his bowl on the great river Euphrates, and its water was dried up, so that the way of the kings from the east might be prepared."

Israel invaded by Iraq because Turkey turns off its water supply? Why not?

They hit Israel within days of the "Desert Storm," and Israel never once retaliated.

Egypt, Ethiopia and Sudan also wrestle with a continual threat of diminishing water supply. Egypt is ninety-five per-cent desert. Isaiah prophesied of Egypt during the final days before the Millennium that,

> The waters will fail from the sea, and the river will be wasted and dried up. The rivers will turn foul, and the brooks of defense will be emptied and dried up; the reeds and rushes will wither. The papyrus reeds by the River [the Nile]...and everything sown by the

River, will wither, be driven away, and be no more. (Isaiah 19:5-7)

The blossoming of the deserts in Israel through irrigation in recent years shows us that water is in fact the key to fulfilling the long-held promises of God to cause the Middle East to blossom again. Forty percent of Israel's fresh water comes from underground water supplies beneath the West Bank and Gaza. Sharing the waters of the Jordan and Yarmuk Rivers keeps tension between Jordan, Syria, and Israel. Israel presently seeks to purchase water from both Lebanon and Turkey, showing also their desperate need for more and more water.

In the light of this reality, how powerful the words of Isaiah become:

> The wilderness and the wasteland shall be glad for them, and the desert shall rejoice and blossom as the rose.... The parched ground shall become a pool, and the thirsty land springs of water; in the habitation of jackals, where each lay, there shall be grass with reeds and rushes. (Isaiah 35:1,7)

Desert is a name applied to regions that are unsuitable for human habitation. There are 56 million square miles of land on the earth. Of this vast region twenty to twenty-five percent is harsh, arid desert. The largest desert in the world, which scientists call the Great Palaearctic Desert, stretches across North Africa and Asia Minor to Northern India and into the heart of China. Southern Africa, Australia, and North and South America also contain desert regions. This means that approximately one-fourth of the earth's land mass is largely non-productive.

According to scientists, the primary cause of deserts is the result of wind patterns, characterized by low rainfall. Wind patterns are so special they have even been assigned descriptive titles. For instance, the North African *khamsin* (from the Arabic word for "50" because it blows for 50 days at a time), creates a thick yellow cloud that reduces visibility to zero. The haboobs of Northern Sudan can limit visibility to a few feet and bring total darkness at high noon. In North America the chubaseos may reach a speed of eighty to one hundred miles per hour.

But the whirlwinds of the desert called "dust devils" form one of the most interesting of phenomenon. On a perfectly still day, when no wind seems to be blowing, a sudden upward rush of heated air lifts sand and other objects from the soil so high into the air that it kills animals, destroys plant life, and relocates surviving things miles away. This is especially interesting in view of John's revelation of a wind-factor phenomenon that is to occur just before the return of Jesus. He writes, "After these things I saw four angels standing at the four corners of the earth, holding the four winds of the earth, that the wind should not blow on the earth, on the sea, or on any tree" (Revelation 7:1).

Imagine the condition of man and beast with no air current flowing to carry away the stifling temperatures that hang over the earth during the last days, when the sun will be seven times hotter. Add to this the possibility of sudden "dust devils" in the Middle East where much of the troubles will be occurring, combined with Turkey's decision to shut off the water of the Euphrates to Syria and Iraq, throwing them into war. Dead bodies, dead fish, dead animals—no water in the Nile for Egypt, Sudan and Ethiopia, Israel under siege, and no air current to relieve the land of its oven-like temperatures—human misery would be intolerable and disease rampant.

According to scientists, there is also another phenomenon that would occur were the winds to cease blowing. To begin with, no sound would be heard if there were no winds to carry it. An eerie silence would suddenly engulf the earth. The heat from the sun would become so hot the rivers and lakes would evaporate.

When night fell, all the moisture that had evaporated would freeze into massive hailstones and fall to the earth. Then, when the sun shone the next day, the intense heat would melt the hailstones and cause massive flooding. Hailstones were used in Egypt. John said they will be used during the First Trumpet (Revelation 8:7), during the Seventh Trumpet (Revelation 11:19), during the Seventh Vial (Revelation 16:17-21), and during Armageddon.

Ezekiel prophesied of the Antichrist who will come against Israel at Armageddon: "And I will bring him to judgment with pestilence and bloodshed; I will rain down on him, on his troops, and on the many peoples who are with him, flooding rain, great hailstones, fire, and brimstone. Thus I will magnify Myself and sanctify Myself, and I will be known in the eyes of many nations. Then they shall know that I am the Lord" (Ezekiel 38:22, 23).

Imagine the squalor of such unbearable conditions and then listen to the words of the prophets:

Zechariah said:

> And it shall be in that day, that living waters shall go out from Jerusalem; half of them toward the former sea [Dead Sea], and half of them toward the hinder sea [Mediterranean]: in summer and in winter shall it be. And the Lord shall be king over all the earth: in that day shall there be one Lord, and his name one. (Zechariah 14:8-9)

It may be that the great earthquake predicted to occur as the Lord sets His feet on the Mount of Olives will surface hidden rivers of water designed into that region just for this occasion. Ezekiel went to great lengths to describe the source and extent of these waters as they come flowing out from under the sanctuary of the Messiah as follows:

> Then he brought me back to the door of the temple; and there was water, flowing from under the threshold of the temple toward the east, for the front of the temple faced east; the water was flowing from under the right side of the temple, south of the altar. He brought me out by way of the north gate, and led me around on the outside to the outer gateway that faces east; and there was water, running out on the right side.
>
> Then, when the man went out to the east with the line in his hand, he measured one thousand cubits, and he brought me through the waters; the water came up to my ankles. Again he measured one thousand and brought me through the waters; the water came up to my knees. Again he measured one thousand and brought me through; the water came up to my waist. Again he measured one thousand, and it was a river that I could not cross; for the water was too deep, water in which one must swim, a river that could not be crossed. He said to me, "Son of man, have you seen this?"
>
> Then he brought me and returned me to the bank of the river. When I returned, there, along the bank of the river, were very many trees on one side and the other. Then he said to me:
>
> "This water flows toward the eastern region, goes down into the valley, and enters the sea. When it reaches the sea, its waters are healed. And it shall be

that every living thing that moves wherever the rivers go, will live. There will be a very great multitude of fish, because these waters go there; for they will be healed, and everything will live wherever the river goes. Along the bank of the river, on this side and that, will grow all kinds of trees used for food; their leaves will not wither, and their fruit will not fail. They will bear fruit every month, because their water flows from the sanctuary. Their fruit will be for food, and their leaves for medicine." (Ezekiel 47:1-9, 12)

The healing of the waters, as in every other act of restoration of the earth, will be a process. The waters that flow out from under Messiah's sanctuary will begin as shallow streams—only ankle deep; they will then rise to the knees; then to the waist; and then they will flow as a river deep enough for swimming.

How long this will take no one knows, but if we go back to Israel's first entrance into Canaan, we will find a principle which God has used throughout human history. God rarely performs His works instantaneously. His plan is to develop at a pace compatible to man's ability to progress. He said to Israel as they were about to enter Canaan, "Don't take the land all at once and destroy the people, lest the wild beasts multiply and overtake the land."

God works by laws—even when He chooses to supersede their usual path with a higher and perhaps faster law—everything God does is "normal," lawful, and completely in harmony with His natural creation. The word "magic" is not a part of God's kingdom. Waters with elements that heal pollution will certainly come from God's laboratory in a manner that we would call miraculous, but scientifically it will make complete sense. After all, the formulas for all things originally came from the mind of the Creator.

Wherever the healing waters of the millennial sanctuary flow, and the healing trees grow, an abundant supply of available medicine will develop until the whole earth is cured of deserts, pollution and disease.

This may well mean that there will be sickness during the Millennium. The practice of medicine will doubtless continue until sin has been conquered and eradicated. Under the new system, however, there will be cures from the trees that always work, and work more quickly. Medicine, as every other institution during this time, is going to advance at a rate it only dreams about now. No longer will men and women sit for twenty or thirty years trying to find a cure for one single virus.

No longer will God's people have to pine away, waiting for a discovery. The healing of the waters to recover the desert areas of the earth will result in the regrowth of magnificent plants that lived on the earth before there was ever a curse. And healthy waters, combined with life-giving vegetation, will enjoy increasing prosperity that will multiply as money multiplies on the exponential curve. One healed today, two tomorrow, then four, then eight, and so forth until health overtakes sickness and life triumphs over death.

Have you every questioned what motivates a person to give his life to searching for cures in our world? Beyond vanity, I believe there is "knowing" inside each person that says, "Disease, deserts, pollution can be conquered!" It is a living witness to the certainty of the Millennium. Saving the planet is not just a dream. In God's time, it will be a reality.

13

An Ointment Poured Forth

Human logic, like rice, is inclined to swell once it is mixed with the intellectual juices of the mind. It can distend the ego and lead man to assume power that does not belong to him. Through logic, secular man has removed the original boundaries of worship. In spite of God's warning to "have no other gods before Me," worship has become a part of man's cultural heritage in the same category with ethnic art and culinary preference.

Sophistication and religious unitarianism have become synonymous in our day. "Every person has a right to choose his own religion." And with this I concur wholeheartedly. Choice of belief is an individual right decreed by the One who sits on the highest courts of the universe. God gave man free choice. But freedom to choose says absolutely nothing about the wisdom of one's choice.

I once ran into three young men at an airport who were so immoral they couldn't even keep their hands off each other in a public place at twelve noon. Never in a million years would I address such a situation alone, naturally speaking. By personality I would run in the opposite direction. But a strength rose up within me and I pointed my index finger toward one of the men in particular, and staring him straight in the eyes, I said, "Jesus loves you. He died so that you could have eternal life!"

"That's right," the young man shot back, "That's why I can do what I want to with my life!" "Wrong!" I fired again, "The love of Jesus is why you're never going to be happy until you turn to Him!" Wrong. What a mean word this has become in our day.

The only "wrong people" today are those who use the word "wrong." But, it is time to remind ourselves that the right to choose, carries no guarantee that it won't be the wrong product. Men can choose to believe whatever they like. They can worship dead men, jade and porcelain figurines, crudely carved demon faces, the heavenly bodies, or the religion of their ancestors. Other men can pretend sophistication and write eloquently about the beauty and complexities of all such beliefs, but in the Millennium men's attitude toward man-made religion is going to change drastically.

God, who is longsuffering, has a very low tolerance for "other gods." Through the prophet Isaiah, God said quite graphically that all religions, outside faith in Him, are like a woman's used sanitary napkin!

Oh yes, He said it. And the millennial man is going to come to that same opinion: "Ye shall defile also the covering of thy graven images of silver, and the ornament of thy molten images of gold: thou shalt cast them away as a menstruous cloth; thou shalt say unto it, Get thee hence" (Isaiah 30:22).

It cuts across the grain, but religious error is headed for hard times. Presently, it is riding the crest of a wave that is rising, but once that wave begins to recede it will fall quickly, never to resurface. Waves are like snowflakes—once they fall, that particular design is gone forever.

The tide of religious error is going out to sea during the Millennium, and it will never again return to pollute the shores of religious truth. The sands of eternity will not be bathed in the waters of religious serendipity. The Millennium will see to that. Beginning at Jerusalem, the truth of one God is going to overtake all false religions so that men themselves will cast away their idols and religious traditions, and set their eyes toward Messiah's sanctuary for their spiritual direction.

> In that day the Branch of the Lord shall be beautiful and glorious; and the fruit of the earth shall be excellent and appealing for those of Israel who have escaped. When the Lord has washed away the filth of the daughters of Zion, and purged the blood of Jerusalem from her midst, by the spirit of judgment and by the spirit of burning, then the Lord will create above every dwelling place of Mount Zion and above her assemblies, a cloud and smoke by day and the shining of a flaming fire by night. For over all the glory there will be a covering. And there will be a tabernacle for shade in the daytime from the heat, for a place of refuge, and for a shelter from storm and rain. (Isaiah 4:2, 4-6)

Doesn't it sound exactly like the presence of Jehovah-Yeshua when He led Israel out of the land of Egypt, by the cloud and the flaming fire? Surely we should all stand to our feet and applaud God for His excellent greatness!

Listen to the words of Paul to the Church:

> Moreover, brethren, I do not want you to be unaware that all our fathers were under the cloud, all passed through the sea, all were baptized into Moses in the cloud and in the sea, all ate the same spiritual food, and all drank the same spiritual drink. For they drank of that spiritual Rock that followed them, and that Rock was Christ. (1 Corinthians 10:1-4)

It's Jesus! Throughout time, when God has appeared to man it has been largely through the second person of the Godhead—Jesus. It was Jesus—the Angel of the Lord—who ministered to Israel under the Old Covenant; it was Jesus—in the form of man—dying to ratify the New Covenant; it is the Spirit of Jesus building the New Covenant Church and empowering it for spiritual works; it will be Jesus ruling the earth from Jerusalem during the millennial restoration. It will always be Jesus—the groom of New Jerusalem—who will wed heaven and earth for eternity.

> Behold what manner of man is this that stands
>   between God and man?
> His eyes are as a flame of fire.
> His fan is in His hand.
> John saw Him in the seven Churches.
> As the sun in brilliancy, behold!
> What manner of man is this?
> What manner of man is He?
>   (A hymn by Phyllis Speers)

There is no God for man but Jesus. Only Jesus has revealed the Father to us. "For it pleased the Father that in Him all the fullness should dwell" (Colossians 1:19).

156

All other religions were birthed out of a man. The Bible tells us clearly that there is one God who created this planet on which we live, and He did it all through His Son Messiah Yeshua, Jesus. Hebrews says of God, "...in these last days he has spoken to us by His Son, whom he appointed heir of all things, and through whom he made the universe. The Son is the radiance of God's glory and the exact repre-sentation of his being, sustaining all things by his powerful Word..." (Hebrews 1:2-3).

This tells you and me that the most we will ever see of God will be in the person Jesus. Jesus himself said it, "If you have seen Me you have seen the Father." I believe God the Father is a personal entity—an individual Person. Yet, the only one who will ever see Him in His full glory will be Yeshua—Jesus. He is the Mediator who has revealed the Father, and will continue to reveal Him. "For there is one God and one Mediator between God and men, the Man Christ Jesus, who gave Himself a ransom for all, to be testified in due time" (1 Timothy 2:5-6).

The Millennium is a time of preparation for the uniting of heaven and earth. It is a time when all creation is being restored and purified for the holy presence of God. But the full glory of God will never be fully discovered except by Jesus and the Holy Spirit. These two—the second and third persons of the Godhead and equal to the Father—will "mediate" or reveal the Father to us throughout eternity.

Do you mean we will never get to see God? I do not mean that exactly. What I am saying is man will never see God in all His glory. How could we? He is infinite, unlimited, above, beyond and out of sight in all His fullness. Even if we looked and probed for ten million years, we would only have begun to discover Him. In order to discover the full glory of God, one would have to be God. To go to the farthest reaches of His infinity, one would have to be infinity. But we can discover Him in and through His Son, who is not only the exact likeness of God but also in the likeness of man.

When you think about it, there is no one in creation quite like Jesus—real God and real Man! Behold what manner of Man is this that stands between us and God? Few of us could comprehend a note from the bank that said, "You have just had a deposit to your account in the sum of eight billion dollars." But once it began to be broken down into tens, twenties, and one hundreds, we would fall right into the flow of its spending power.

Even so, Jesus is the person through whom the glory of God is broken down into rays of obtainable reflections. Jesus makes it possible to get hold of the infinite God in a way we can understand.

His Name—An Ointment

It is written of Jesus, "Thy name is as ointment poured forth" (Song of Solomon 1:3).

Archaeologists digging in Israel recently found a bottle of oil 2,000 years old. They are convinced it was the type of oil used for anointing the ancient priests of God. And do you know what the consistency of that oil was? It was not thin and watery so that it evaporated quickly. It was not hard and dry so that it could not be applied. It was not rancid and objectionable so that no one would desire it. The anointing oil was thick, fragrant, heavy, sticky and gooey like honey. This tells us that once the anointing oil was poured out upon the head of the ancient priest, it ran down slowly, deliberately, full-bodied—sticking closely to its subject. Oozing from the crown, to the ears, over the eyes to the lips, to the beard, to the chest and the heart, across the shoulders to the fingertips, over the loins, to the thighs—and dripping down from the hem of the robe, it dropped upon the feet in sticky mounds. (See Psalm 133:2.)

Three times the Scripture declares: "How beautiful upon the mountains are the feet of him that bringeth good tidings, that publisheth peace; that bringeth good tidings of good, that publisheth salvation; that saith unto Zion, Thy God reigneth!" (Isaiah 52:7).

Of course the feet of the believers are beautiful. They carry the good tidings of a gooey, fragrant Name that takes hold of a life and sticks closer than a brother, and seeps down into the very pores of the innermost being, with an anointing that releases the very presence of the Father.

Jesus said "Whatsoever ye shall ask the Father in my name, he may give it you... Hitherto have ye asked nothing in my name: ask, and ye shall receive, that your joy may be full" (John 15:16; 16:24).

Of all the great restorations to come during the kingdom era, none will compare to the reverence that is going to be restored to the name of Yeshua, Jesus. In the world His name is scorned and taken lightly; in the Church it is sorely underestimated; but in the realm of the spirit the name of Jesus has utmost respect. Demons know its strength, angels rejoice in its authority, and for 1,000 years, the earth and the Church are going to be taught to appreciate its full-bodied power.

For 2,000 years, the Church has occupied itself with making the name of Jesus known. In the Millennium, the Church will get to know the Name.

It was a common belief of antiquity that a name was not simply a label but an actual part of the personality of the one who bore it. Using the name of a god or a person actually called that god or person into the situation. Using the name of Jesus brings Jesus onto the scene. If His name is used in vain, then His personal weight falls on the guilty one who has profaned it.

"You shall not take the name of the Lord your God in vain; for the Lord will not hold him guiltless who takes His name in vain." On the other hand, His name used in reverence brings His personal authority to bear on that situation with blessing.

We know the principle and we say it, but we have yet to know The Name. God promises to hear when properly called upon, but His name is a gift of revelation. God revealed His name to Abraham (Genesis 17:1) and Moses (Exodus 6:2). And what He revealed was not a code number but a living, active presence.

Listen to what God instructed Israel as they were preparing to possess Canaan:

> But when you cross over the Jordan and dwell in the land which the Lord your God is giving you to inherit, and when He gives you rest from all your enemies round about, so that you dwell in safety, then there will be the place where the Lord your God chooses to make His name abide. (Deuteronomy 12:10)

God's name, the name of His Son—is a living presence that demands the same reverence as His person would command if He stood visibly before us. Canaan would have been impossible to possess, had not the name of Jehovah been living with Israel, taking the victory in the spirit realm.

As the end of the ages comes upon the world, the name of Jesus will begin to be revealed to the saints of God once again, both Jew and Gentile. And with that revelation we will stand for the Lord in the hottest part of the battle, without retreat. It is one of the three living presence He promised the Church—His Name, His Word and His Spirit. It is with these that we will sweep into the Millennium with a power that will cause even the giants to bow down and confess His superiority.

Bowing to the Name

When Scripture says that "at the name of Jesus every knee should bow, of things in heaven...earth...and under the earth, and that every tongue should confess that [Yeshua Ha Mashiach] Jesus Christ is Lord" (Philippians 2:10-11), it does not mean to imply that all creation will one day, reluctantly slither down on one knee and mutter, "Okay, I concede. "

There is a day coming when every thing that has breath will realize with full cognizance that Jesus truly is Lord of creation. Their knees—our knees—will bend from the sheer weight of truth finally dawning upon us.

Earthly royalty protects the honor of the names of royalty by allowing themselves to be referred to only in the third person—Her majesty, Queen Elizabeth. An honor far superior to this will one day rise from the breast of every man, woman, and child as they handle the revealed Name of Jesus as a piece of the thinnest crystal.

Ancient Israel set the example for us "on whom the ends of the world are come" The priests of God took Scripture and in a small piece of leather bound the Word of God to their forehead. These pieces were called frontlets. Moses wrote to the men of Israel:

"And these words which I command you today shall be in your heart... you shall bind them as a sign on your hand, and they shall be as frontlets between your eyes" (Deuteronomy 6:6-8). This command of God was doubtless in preparation for the Millennium—when all believers will wear, not simply a portion of the written word, but the Name of the Living Word as frontlets between our eyes. John said, "His name shall be on their [our] foreheads" (Revelation 22:4).

The revelation of the absolute authority and glory of Jesus' name is destined to be revealed in the coming kingdom. We will all wear it proudly as a fragrant ointment poured out upon our own lives. It will be a mark of royalty.

14

Forty Days into the Future
(Resurrection Man)

Jesus was not the first to experience resurrection from the dead. At least eight other persons preceded Him in returning from the underworld.

Some 1500 years before the Resurrection of Jesus took place, a band of Moabites invaded Israel. At one point, when they needed to dispose of a body quickly, they unwittingly threw it into the tomb of the prophet Elisha. The moment the body touched the prophet's bones, the man was resurrected and came back to life. Elisha was the prophet who himself had invaded death with the restoration of a Shunamite woman's young son. (See 2 Kings chapter 4.)

During Jesus' brief ministry of three and a half years, He did not hesitate to use the resurrection power to reverse the death process and bring back a young girl (Mark 5:38-43), a young man (Luke 7:14), and His close friend Lazarus (John 11).

The resurrection is a fact as old as the Bible. Job, considered by many to be the oldest of the sixty-six books, taught it saying, "For I know that my redeemer liveth, and that he shall stand at the latter day upon the earth: And though after my skin worms destroy this body, yet in my flesh shall I see God: Whom I shall see for myself, and mine eyes shall behold, and not another; though my reins be consumed within me" (Job 19:25-27).

The fact being stated and substantiated by eight previous examples, what then makes the resurrection of Jesus so special? What does His resurrection reveal that other seemingly similar accounts do not? The answer is obvious, but amazing. It is a new depth of understanding that makes the skin itch for the Millennium.

The distance between God and man, this world and the other sphere, is much closer than we imagine. The natural world is not foreign to God. He created it as surely as heaven was created. In Genesis 1:31 we read that, "God saw every thing that he had made, and, behold, it was very good...."

If we will ever understand the future, as well as, present implications of the resurrection, we must dispel the notion that God dislikes this natural world and, along with it, our physical bodies.

When I growing up, it was common to hear people say, "Never mind this old body; when I die just throw me in a ditch somewhere." My mother would always respond, "No. The body is sacred and deserves respect!"

She was right, of course. All creation is potentially beautiful and eternal. The patriarch Joseph's dying request was to carry his bones back to Canaan when Israel was set free from slavery in Egypt. It was a long, hot journey that would take forty years, but Joseph wanted his physical remains in place, not for the sake of the past but for the future. Joseph sensed the millennial resurrection.

Perhaps it is important to notice, for those who have difficulty believing in something as miraculous as a resurrection of the body, that the Resurrection of Jesus took place and was being preached before one word of the Gospels or Paul's Epistles was written.

The New Testament was written after and in view of the fact of the resurrection. If you can believe the historical accounts of Jesus' ministry in Matthew, Mark, Luke and John, and if you can accept the wisdom of Jesus' social and moral philosophy, then why not remain open to the possibility of a unique return from the abyss of death that has changed the world forever?

Historically, the world has always held one of two views concerning life after death: either we become nothing, or we take another form after death which no one has yet been able to describe. As C.S. Lewis wrote, "We feel quite sure that the first step beyond the world of our present experience must lead either nowhere at all or else into the blinding abyss of undifferentiated spirituality...." In other words, we are either nothing or we are a shapeless, faceless spiritual mist. Lewis goes on to conclude, "That is why many believe in God who cannot believe in angels and an angelic world. That is why many believe in immortality who cannot believe in the resurrection of the body... and why many desire a Christianity stripped of its miracles" (C.S. Lewis. *Miracles*. New York, NY: Macmillan Publishing Co., Inc. 1960, p. 163).

A Christianity that no longer has miracles is a Christianity that has stopped the resurrection power dead in its tracks. The full purpose of the resurrection is yet to be accomplished in the lives of the members of the Body of Christ.

The Apostle Paul tried to tell us this when he declared that his greatest desire was to know Christ "and the power of his resurrection" (Philippians 3:10). Paul knew that the resurrection had a work yet to be accomplished, and that its work had everything to do with his own personal destiny.

The cross, the Resurrection, and the Ascension are not a three-part, divine event that took place once upon a time in history, and all who believe in this event will have some kind of vague, unidentifiable future awaiting them somewhere. Quite the contrary.

Calvary, the Resurrection, and the Ascension served to activate a plan that is older than creation. They set in motion God's original design for bringing time back into harmony with eternity—where death is totally and finally swallowed up by immortality.

Appearances After the Resurrection

To understand this great mystery, let us go back for a moment to the scene of Jesus' resurrection. The apostle John records in chapters twenty and twenty-one several events that took place on the third day following Jesus' burial.

The first event occurred when Mary Magdalene went to the tomb and discovered that it was empty. Looking through the door and weeping Mary saw two angels who said, "...Woman, why weepest thou? She saith unto them, Because they have taken away my Lord, and I know not where they have laid him. And when she had thus said, she turned herself back, and saw Jesus standing, and knew not that it was Jesus" (John 20:13-14).

As the story continued, Mary recognized that the man talking to her was Jesus.

The second appearance of Jesus happened as the disciples, with the exception of Thomas, sat behind locked doors for fear of unbelievers. Suddenly Jesus stood in their midst and said, "Peace be unto you" (John 20:19). Then He showed them the marks of the crucifixion in His hands and side and confirmed that He was still flesh and bones.

> And He said to them, "Why are you troubled? And why do doubts arise in your hearts?" Behold My hands and My feet, that it is I Myself. Handle Me and see, for a spirit does not have flesh and bones as you see I have." When He had said this, He showed them His hands and His feet. But while they still did not believe for joy, and marveled, He said to them, "Have you any food here?" So they gave Him a piece of a broiled fish and some honeycomb. And He took it and ate in their presence. (Luke 24: 38-43)

Eight days later, Jesus again appeared to the disciples with Thomas present. Exposing the marks of His crucifixion, doubting Thomas said, "My Lord and my God" (John 20:28).

On another occasion, two men were walking on the road to Emmaus discussing all the events surrounding the crucifixion when Jesus suddenly joined them. He then explained all that the prophets had written concerning His death and resurrection. Not recognizing Him, the two men urged Jesus to come in for the evening. As they sat down to eat, their eyes were suddenly opened and He vanished out of their sight. (See Luke 24:31.)

An Ointment Poured Forth Again. The disciples were in Galilee where they had been fishing all night. When morning came, Jesus stood on the shore and called out to them about their catch, but they did not recognize Him. He then told them where to cast their nets for a deluge of fish. Shortly thereafter, they came to shore where they all sat down together and ate grilled fish and bread.

As they sat eating together, Jesus said to Peter,

> Simon, son of Jonas, do you have a love for me
> called out of your heart by my preciousness to you,
> a devotional love that im-pels you to sacrifice your-
> self for me? Do you consider me more precious and
> thus love me more than these [fish]? He says to Him,
> yes, Lord, as for you, you know positively that I have
> an emotional fondness for you. He says to him, Be
> feeding my little lambs. (John 21:15, Wuest, The New
> Testament Expanded Translation)

Twice more, Jesus pressured Peter with the subject of love for God and people. But what does all this tell us? Were the appearances of Jesus after His death simply to prove that He had in fact conquered death? Or was there something more added to these glorious post resurrection visits?

I believe there was something much more than a proof factor involved in those forty days. There was, in fact, a demonstration going on. Jesus' various appearances on the earth following His resurrection were not only to confirm the success of His appointment at Calvary with Satan, but Jesus demonstrated for the first time on the earth the future state of all believers.

Paul wrote, "But now is Christ risen from the dead, and become the firstfruits of them that slept" (2 Corinthians 15:20). But since we know that at least eight other mortals had been resurrected prior to Jesus, His resurrection had to contain something different. And it did. His was the first of a kind to ever appear on earth.

And what was that kind? Jesus demonstrated immortal man! Glorified humanity! In His resurrection body,

Jesus demonstrated what the true man of the future is going to be like. His was the first glimpse of the future state of the millennial resurrected saints!

Church, we need to stop wondering what we are going to look like, be like, and do in the Millennium. Jesus has given us a preview. We need to stop fearing extinction at death—stop imagining that we will never see our loved ones again, that at best we will float in a meaningless spiritual state of non-productivity forever. Jesus has already shown us what we can expect.

"For the Lord himself shall descend from heaven with a shout, with the voice of the archangel, and with the trump of God: and the dead in Christ shall rise first" (1 Thessalonians 4:16).

And what shall we be like? Let's review the pattern:

- Resurrected Jesus had flesh and bones.
- He ate.
- He talked and fellowshiped with His old friends.
- He was recognizable.
- He even engaged in the business of catching fish.
- He had power to reveal more understanding of God.
- He had memory.
- He was not subject to natural laws and limitations of the flesh as in His natural state.
- He could travel between heaven and earth without a vehicle.
- He could appear and disappear at will.
- He could do signs, wonders, and miracles. That is, He had total dominion over nature.
- He was active in the Father's business.
- He brought peace wherever He went.
- He pursued love of God and man.

In the shadow of the cross there has always been the light of the Resurrection. The Church is in training now for its glorified state of immortality!

God never intended man to be a powerless, defeated mortal. His original intention was not that we be mortal at all. How could it be when we are created in His eternal image?

We were designed to have dominion authority, miracle working power coursing through our eternal veins. And, as Jesus demonstrated, we are designed to flow with that divine image here on earth.

We should and we can even now if...we understand that everything of ourselves, both natural and spiritual, belongs to God.

The body of man is destined for the Millennium. Everything about our times declares it.

In recent years there has been a surge of something new in the Church. It has tried to express itself in numerous ways—through praise and worship, even the arts. Some call it emotionalism, and they try to tame it with the whip of tradition and get it back in line.

But nothing will be able to stop what God is doing. He is preparing man to release His body—as David released his body when he leaped and danced before the ark of the Lord with all his might. In the midst of all the restoration that is coming, the body, soul, and spirit of man are destined to enjoy a liberty of celebration unlike anything we have ever enjoyed in this natural world.

The time is near! Satan would not be flooding the world with a counterfeit "liberation" of the body based on immorality, gender and a hundred other "causes" if it were not so. Satan and the spirit world understand the hour better than the Church. They are saying to the people, " Let loose! Let your body free to enjoy itself!" It is perverted, but a thread of truth is in this mad rush to liberation! The bodies of the human race are on the verge of being "set free."

For 6,000 years we have had on the grave clothes of the first Adam. But the day is soon coming when we will shed this dying shroud for an immortal, white linen garment that will never get sick, die nor decay.

The new liberty of the body in worship and praise— lifting the hands, clapping, dancing, shouting before the Lord are in preparation for the advancing kingdom.

God is taking control of His creation—including nature. As C.S. Lewis has said,

> To shrink back from all that can be called Nature into negative spirituality is as if we ran away from horses instead of learning to ride. 'Who will trust us with the true wealth if we cannot be trusted even with the wealth that perishes?' Who will trust me with a spiritual body if I cannot control even an earthly body?
>
> These small and perishable bodies we now have were given to us as ponies are given to schoolboys. We must learn to manage: not that we may some day be free of horses altogether but that some day we may ride bare-back, confident and rejoicing, those greater mounts, those winged, shining and world-shaking horses which perhaps even now expect us with impatience, pawing and snorting in the King's stables. Not that the gallop would be of any value unless it were a gallop with the King; but how else—since He has retained His own charger—should we accompany Him?" (C.S. Lewis. *Miracles*. New York, NY: Macmillan Publishing Co., 1960, p. 163.)

171

There is only one way to ride with Jesus, and that is to bring all of nature and all of spirit into the flow of His resurrection power. The Apostle Paul longed for the day when he could ride freely with the One on the front charger. Until that day, however, he rode with all the power available to triumphantly finish his course and keep the faith.

Other men have risen from the dead only to die again. But Jesus was the first to become eternal man in full splendor! That same resurrection is working in every one of us right now toward that moment of our own transformation!

For forty days, Jesus walked the earth after His resurrection, giving believers a glimpse of their own glorious destiny in the Millennium. "For the earnest expectation of the creature waiteth for the manifestation of the sons of God" (Romans 8:19).

15

Ruling and Reigning
on the Earth

We know where the Jews will be during the Millennium—they will be gathered from the four corners of the earth to live in Israel. God said He would send fishers out to catch and draw them back home to their land. We know where the resurrected saints will be during the Millennium—they will be priests and kings, the manifested sons of God on divine assignment dispatched among the nations.

But where will the natural Gentiles be located? Those who are alive at the coming of Jesus?

According to the writing of Moses, which was quoted by Paul in the book of Acts, the original division of the earth took place with the three sons of Noah. "These were the families of the sons of Noah, according to their generations, in their nations, and from these the nations were divided on the earth after the flood" (Genesis 10:32).

Moses picked up on this statement later in Deuteronomy with further clarification, saying, "When the Most High divided their inheritance to the nations, when He separated the sons of Adam, He set the boundaries of the peoples according to the number of the children of Israel" (Deuteronomy 32:8).

In other words, God placed the descendants of Isaac in the land of the future capital of the earth where Messiah will rule and set government policy for the nations. But the rest of the earth He apportioned to the Gentiles. During the Millennium, the Gentile nations that survive God's purging will continue to live and operate as natural people—working, building, marrying, and rearing families. With the advance of time, they will be radically altered in lifestyle, but they will be natural nations just as they are natural today—driving cars to work, taking planes, applying for jobs, continuing with education.

In all nations, civil and religious laws will be mandatory. Isaiah said,

> Now it shall come to pass in the latter days that the mountain of the Lord's house shall be established on the top of the mountains, and shall be exalted above the hills; and all nations shall flow to it. Many people shall come and say, 'Come, and let us go up to the mountain of the Lord, to the house of the God of Jacob; He will teach us His ways, and we shall walk in His paths.' For out of Zion shall go forth the law, and the word of the Lord from Jerusalem. He shall judge between the nations, and shall rebuke many people; they shall beat their swords into plowshares, and their spears into pruning hooks; nation shall not lift up sword against nation, neither shall they learn war anymore. (Isaiah 2:2-4)

Jesus is going to teach the nations how to settle their differences peacefully. His policies are going to transform man's understanding of what it takes to prosper at living. But natural life will continue.

The procedure by which the Gentiles will be governed on a national level is not spelled out clearly in the Scriptures. According to John's revelation, the Church will be placed in charge of the Gentile Nations, under Messiah. "And he who overcomes, and keeps My works until the end, to him I will give power over the nations—'He shall rule them with a rod of iron; as the potter's vessels shall be broken to pieces'—as I also have received from My Father" (Revelation 2:26,27).

Mortal Gentiles, those who are alive at Jesus' coming, will doubtless have a role in governing themselves as well. We know this from Zechariah's warning of punishment upon the Gentile Nations that do not send representatives to Jerusalem each year during the Feast of Tabernacles.

> And it shall come to pass that everyone who is left of all the nations which came against Jerusalem shall go up from year to year to worship the King, the Lord of hosts, and to keep the Feast of Tabernacles. And it shall be that whichever of the families of the earth do not come up to Jerusalem to worship the King, the Lord of hosts, on them there will be no rain. If the family of Egypt will not come up and enter in, they shall have no rain; they shall receive the plague with which the Lord strikes the nations who do not come up to keep the Feast of Tabernacles. (Zechariah 14:16-19)

This also confirms again the fact that there will be unbelievers during the Millennium who will refuse to obey God's laws.

Internationally, Jesus will rule the nations. He will be the King of kings. He will head up the central government of the entire world population. But on a national scale, nations will continue to have their regional leadership. Jesus will rule under God. Kings will rule under Jesus—answering yearly to the King of kings.

For example, Scripture is quite clear about the future government of the nation Israel. In at least four places, Scripture teaches that at the Second Coming of Messiah with the saints, David will be the one raised up to sit on the throne of Israel as a prince under Him. More than once I have visited the tomb of David in Jerusalem. I consider it a sacred place, because one day the king's body will come out of its encasement and rise to the royal occasion!

Now these are the words that the Lord spoke concerning Israel and Judah. "For it shall come to pass in the day," says the Lord of hosts, that I will break his yoke from your neck, and will burst your bonds; foreigners shall no more enslave them. But they shall serve the Lord their God, and David their king, whom I will raise up for them" (Jeremiah 30:4,8-9).

Again, Ezekiel says, "And I, the Lord, will be their God, and My servant David a prince among them; I, the Lord, have spoken" (Ezekiel 34:24).

But no one paints the picture more clearly than Hosea when he says, "For the children of Israel shall abide many days without king or prince, without sacrifice or sacred pillar, without ephod or teraphim. Afterward the children of Israel shall return, seek the Lord their God and David their king, and fear the Lord and His goodness in the latter days" (Hosea 3:4,5).

Has Israel been many days without a king? Almost 2,000 years. Have they been without the prescribed sacrifice? Have their priests been without their holy garments? The Millennium is going to restore it all.

Jesus, the Messiah, will rule under God. King David will rule under Jesus, and under David will be the twelve apostles. Yes, the apostles will rule one over each of the twelve tribes of Israel.

Peter once went to Jesus and questioned, "...See, we have left all and followed You. Therefore what shall we have? So Jesus said to them, "Assuredly I say to you, that in the regeneration [restoration], when the Son of Man sits on the throne of His glory, you who have followed Me will also sit on twelve thrones, judging the twelve tribes of Israel" (Matthew 19:27-28).

As my friend Carol Duhart pointed out, upon hearing this truth, "Then Jesus knew when He was calling His disciples to follow Him that their calling would reach all the way into the Millennium!" And she's right.

Lest anyone should get the idea here of reincarnation, what Jesus was explaining to Peter was not reincarnation but resurrection. At the coming of Jesus to earth, the bodies of all believers will be resurrected into an immortal state to be reunited with their soul and spirit forever. This means that the earth will have both mortal and immortal residents living on it. We will work and interact with each other just as Jesus and His disciples interacted with each other after His resurrection.

Reincarnation is actually a perverted form of the truth. However misdirected, it demonstrates the hunger in man's heart for immortality. During the Millennium, millions in the Far East who have been held in bondage to this religious error are going to be released to the knowledge of truth about immortality.

"But why," you may ask, "will people believe then who reject the truth now with fanatical opposition?" The answer lies in an event that will take place at the coming of Jesus, when His armies defeat Satan and his legions. Do you recall when Jesus was crucified, how He went into hell, confronted Satan, and took the keys of death and hell from him? From that point on, Jesus has retained the authority to lock up or release from hell whomever He chooses. John writes in Revelation,

> Then I saw an angel coming down from heaven, having the key to the bottomless pit and a great chain in his hand. He laid hold of the dragon, that serpent of old, who is the Devil and Satan, and bound him for a thousand years; and he cast him into the bottomless pit, and shut him up, and set a seal on him, so that he would deceive the nations no more till the thousand years were finished. But after these things he must be released for a little while. (Revelation 20:1-3)

Millions in the Far East and all over the earth will come to the knowledge of truth during the Millennium because Satan will be bound from directly influencing their lives. At the battle of Armageddon, when Jesus comes to rescue Israel, Satan is going to be bound from operating on the earth for one thousand years. Understand something, Satan will not be destroyed—spirit cannot be killed. That is why no person ever vanishes into nothingness. Spirit is eternal.

Satan is spirit; he will never be destroyed. He will, however, be bound from operating in God's kingdom realm for 1,000 years, after which time he will be loosed to expose any rebellion that still exists on earth. John writes, "Now when the thousand years have expired, Satan will be released from his prison and will go out to deceive the nations which are in the four corners of the earth, Gog and

Magog, to gather them together to battle, whose number is as the sand of the sea" (Revelation 20:7,8).

Amazingly, after 1,000 years of revival, in a world of peace and prosperity, millions of people will still be rebellious against God and His authority over their lives. They will continue to resent the Kingdom constitution and standards. It is difficult to understand, but some people would rather be miserable than bow down to God. John said the number of the rebellious will be "as the sand of the sea." That is a vast host, a host so set on pride that they will try once again to defeat righteousness.

These will be people who are as sick of holiness as we are of ungodliness today. They will be people who hold their ears in the malls (as we hold ours now), because they are sick to death of the lyrics that badger their souls. This ungodly host of people from the four corners of the earth will join with Satan at the end of the thousand years, and make war once again on Israel. But this time Israel will not even have to fire up their shiny jet fighters. God will have been monitoring the whole build-up.

Though done in secret, once the armies of Satan are well-positioned around Israel and Jerusalem, ready to attack, God will intervene supernaturally. John said:

> ...fire came down from God out of heaven and devoured them. And the devil that deceived them was cast into the lake of fire and brimstone, where the beast and false prophet are [and have been there for one thousand years already. Remember, they were cast into the lake at the beginning of the Millennium], and shall be tormented day and night forever. (Revelation 20:9,10)

Satan will not die, but forever he will be confined to the caverns at the center of the earth, among the molten lava and miserable hosts who followed him there—all of which brings us to our final group of earthlings whose bodies have been sleeping in the dust since their death. These are the unbelievers who were not resurrected at the coming of Jesus. They did not awaken to enjoy the millennial restoration of all the earth. They did not see the waters healed, animals restored, and the heavens light up like a Christmas celebration. They did not live to see justice restored in the courts, governments cleaned up, diseases healed and people live for hundreds of years, free from fear of death. And they did not live to enjoy true worship of God where people advance from one celebration to another.

The Great White Throne

John said of the unbelieving dead,

> Then I saw a great white throne and Him who sat on it, from whose face the earth and the heaven fled away. And there was found no place for them. And I saw the dead, small and great, standing before God, and books were opened. And another book was opened which is the Book of Life. And the dead were judged according to their works by the things which were written in the books. The sea gave up the dead who were in it, and Death and Hades delivered up the dead who were in them. And they were judged, each one according to his works.(Revelation 20:11-13)

No saints will be standing at the White Throne Judgment. Only those whose names are no longer recorded in that most precious of books. Certainly history has record of no sadness to compare with the moment when two longing eyes search frantically for a name that has been erased by its own doubt and unbelief—and that person finds his name—her name—forever missing from the Book of Life.

"And anyone not found written in the Book of Life was cast into the lake of fire" (Revelation 20:15).

Unbelievers only will stand at the Great White Throne Judgment of God. Their day in court will not be to determine if they shall be invited to live in God's kingdom, this judgment was sealed at the moment of their natural death. "It is appointed unto men once to die but after this the judgment" (Hebrews 9:27).

What the unbeliever will be judged for will be his evil works here on earth. I believe there are degrees or compartments in the underworld of greater and lesser torments. The Bible teaches that hell is:

- located beneath the ocean floor (Job 26:5,6).

- divided into five departments: tartarus (1 Peter 3:19); "paradise" which was emptied when Jesus arose from death with his saints (Luke 16:19-31); hell (Matthew 16:18); the abyss or bottomless pit (Luke 8:26-31); the lake of fire (Revelation 20:6, 11-15).

- a place of pain and sorrow (Psalm 18:51; 116:3).

The Great White Throne Judgment will determine where—in which compartment—the unbeliever and ungodly will spend eternity. But regardless where the lost reside, it will be a place of pain and sorrow. And just in case any of the redeemed should even be tempted to turn back from eternity, Isaiah said there will be an opening where we can look into hell as a continual warning against sin:

"And they shall go forth and look upon the corpses of the men who have transgressed against Me. For their worm does not die, and their fire is not quenched. They shall be an abhorrence to all flesh" (Isaiah 66:24).

At the end of the Millennium, in eternity, there will be three classes of men: the lost who are condemned to the underworld; the natural saved who are the subjects of God's kingdom; and the resurrected saints who are rulers of the kingdom. These three classes will be forever.

In the final chapter of this book, I want us to turn our eyes to the God of eternity and the purpose for all things. I want us to end this glimpse of the Millennium on the first note of—forever. And that note is celebrate!

16

Celebrate!

Tisha be-Av is a day of fasting set aside by the Jewish people to commemorate their sorrows. Av, the fifth month on the Jewish calendar corresponds to July/August. It is not a day officially called by God, but one called by the people to commemorate the burning of their first and second temples—in 586 B.C. by the Babylonians and A.D. 70 by the Romans.

Jeremiah records that " in the fifth month, in the tenth day of the month...came Nebuzaradan...which served the king of Babylon...and burned the house of the Lord, and the king's house; and all the houses of Jerusalem, and all the houses of the great men, burned he with fire" (Jeremiah 52:12- 13).

Some fifty years later, however, God spoke to Zechariah the prophet saying that Tisha be-Av and the three additional fasts of Israel were destined to be turned into feasts! " ...The fast of the fourth month, and the fast of the fifth, and the fast of the seventh, and the fast of the tenth, shall be to the house of Judah joy and gladness, and cheerful feasts; therefore love the truth and peace" (Zechariah 8:19).

The Millennium will not be a time of fasting, but a time of feasting and celebration. Fasting has always been a significant part of the believer's life. The disciples of John once came to Jesus inquiring about the fact that His disciples did not keep the traditional fasts of Israel. And Jesus answered them by saying, "Can the children of the bridegroom mourn, as long as the bridegroom is with them? but the days will come, when the bridegroom shall be taken from them, and then shall they fast" (Matthew 9:15).

Now is the time to fast and sacrifice our lives for the sake of the gospel. Now is the time to discipline our flesh and keep it chaste and sensitive to the voice of the Holy Spirit. Now is the time to plant and work the fields. The time is coming when the Master of the house will return with rewards and celebration on His mind. Then will our talents be assessed, our works examined for spiritual content, and dividends paid according to commission.

On a high mountain in the vicinity of Jerusalem, a spacious, thirty-four-square mile area will one day house the millennial temple of Messiah. Out of His sanctuary will flow the divine order of government and worship for Israel and all nations. The schedule for the special celebrations will be issued and observed on the calendar, even as we observe special times and seasons today.

All "fast" days will be turned into feasting. All "feast" days will be reinstituted to the fulfilling of their original intention.

Celebrate!

Just the sound of the word lifts the heart. Holidays get special recognition on every calendar, because the word holiday was originally a "Holy Day" set aside for worship and the refreshing of the total person.

Under the Old Covenant with Israel, God set aside certain calendar days for feasting. With the flood of Babylonian influence in the early church at Rome, however, the western church largely forgot the feasts of Jehovah and instituted in their place a Christianized version of pagan holidays—such as Easter, the pagan worship of Astarte, instead of Passover, and All Saint's Day on Halloween when demonic lords were worshiped, instead of the Feast of Tabernacles when the harvest was gathered in and Jehovah was praised.

By and large, the Church is only vaguely familiar with the feasts of God. Yet, the Apostle Paul, in writing to the church, said: "Let no man therefore judge you...in respect of an holy day, or of the new moon, or of the sabbath days: Which are a shadow of things to come...." (Colossians 2:16).

The ancient feasts given to Israel are "a shadow of things to come." They are the special days certain to be printed on the calendars of the Millennium. They are days we should dust off now and begin to anticipate.

In the book of Leviticus, chapter 23, we find a complete list of the eight feasts to which the Apostle Paul referred. They are the:

- Weekly Sabbath
- Feast of Passover
- Unleavened Bread

185

- Firstfruits
- Feast of Pentecost
- Feast of Tabernacles
- Feast of Trumpets
- Feast of Atonement

If we go back, we will also find that as God began to instruct Israel about the feasts, He told them that, "...it shall be a statute forever...."

The word forever is the Hebrew word *olam* and means: vanishing point, time out of mind, eternity, perpetual, at any time, beginning of the world without end.

The eight feasts of God are perpetual, at all times, without end, and they hold great significance for the believer in the days to come.

Therefore, as we look briefly at these feasts, we are not looking back in order to gain information—but we are looking ahead in order to gain revelation as to what we can expect in the way of millennial celebrations.

Moreover, since God's purpose for establishing the feasts and special holy days began with the Sabbath rest, why don't we start there.

Does heaven observe Sabbath?

Will eternity observe Sabbath?

Since He never gets tired (Isaiah 40:28), why did God rest after He had created the world?

Did you know that God rested on the seventh day approximately 2,550 years before He made it a law for His people?

For the most part, God's people have always reduced spiritual things to natural terms. Whereas, sabbath has now come to mean "a time to rest your mind and body from the routine of work," its spiritual intention is far greater.

The Bible tells us that Sabbaths range from:

1 day (Exodus 16:23-29)
2 days (Leviticus 23:6-8)
1 year (Leviticus 25:4)
70 years (2 Chronicles 36:21)
Eternity (Hebrews 4:9)

Avoiding the snare of legalism about which day is the true Sabbath, the issue remains: Sabbath is spiritual. It is an eternal observance, and it is for the Church as well as for Israel.

Sabbath began in heaven. The first day God rested from natural work, Sabbath went eternally into effect.

When God created man, He immediately established a relationship with him. Everything God spoke to Adam was either a natural or a divine commission. Adam lived in a "daily Sabbath" relationship with God. In the mornings he went about his natural duties; in the afternoons he stopped everything and fellowshiped with God. Without doubt, on the seventh day of each week, God and Adam spent most of the day together.

Every other feast of God comes out of the Sabbath framework. Sabbath is as simple as God's desire to fellowship with His man, created in His image, modeled after His likeness, and capable of His same desires. It is as complicated as man's desperate need to continually draw life from his Creator through the "life line" of worship.

God wants us to *live*; we want to *live*—only worship makes this possible. Therefore a time of worship has been eternally established. Every other feast is a Sabbath of worship—a time set aside for God and man.

> "For as the new heavens and the new earth which I will make shall remain before Me," says the Lord, "so shall your descendants and your name remain. And it shall come to pass that from one New Moon to another, and from one Sabbath to another, all flesh shall come to worship before Me," says the Lord. (Isaiah 66:22-23)

The Millennium will observe the Sabbath days and keep the feasts of God. And when you stop to consider, it all makes complete sense. Who cannot see the eternal significance of Passover, Pentecost, and Tabernacles?

Passover (*Pecach*)

Passover is the festival of redemption. It began the moment in eternity when Jesus agreed to take human form and shed his blood for the sins of man. First Peter 1:2 says that Jesus' blood is forever "sprinkling" forgiveness in the sanctuary of heaven. Israel observed the shed blood of Jesus through animal sacrifices under the Old Covenant.

They will resume these sacrifices as a memorial offering during the Millennium, (see Ezekiel 46), just as the Church has and will continue to take the bread and wine of the Lord's Supper. There will never be a time when man will forget the great price paid for his salvation. Even throughout eternity the Passover will be celebrated.

The original celebration of Passover was preceded by the farmers going through their fields and marking the best of their crops as "firstfruits." On the morning of Nisan 16, at the Feast of Passover, the "firstfruits" were presented to the Lord. One portion of the offering was waved before the Lord by the priest and a small amount was burned upon the altar—which tells us that the worship of God with our tithes and offerings is also an eternal ordinance that will continue into eternity.

There will never be a time when the law of giving to God will be rescinded. Giving is not simply a financial strategy to supply God's house, but it is a part of the divine nature that keeps the life-flow of God moving within His people. It is the divine key to a healthy soul as well as a healthy economy.

In addition to the giving of "firstfruits", Passover was a time of purification and cleansing. All leaven (representing the world) was removed from the home and only unleavened bread was eaten. The celebration of "Unleavened Bread" prepares us for the time when we will lay aside all the worries, all the cares, all the strivings of natural achievements and we will enter into God's Sabbath of spiritual works. It will be a celebration of effort without ego and fruitfulness without ungodly frustration.

Pentecost (*Shavuoth*-Feast of Weeks)

Pentecost commemorates the giving of the law at Sinai—the Old Covenant. It pointed to the coming of the Holy Spirit to establish a New Covenant when God would write His word upon our hearts (See Hebrews 8:10). As the "former rain" of the Spirit fell, the New Covenant with the Church went into effect and men received the Holy Spirit in their hearts.

At the Second Coming of Jesus, the "latter rains" will fall and all Israel will be reborn along with many Gentile nations. Throughout the Millennium, then, the Holy Spirit will write upon the hearts of men all the wisdom and power they need for living.

Feast of Tabernacles (*Succot*)

The Feast of Tabernacles begins two weeks after *Rosh Hashanah*—the celebration of the New Year, also known as the Feast of Trumpets. The greetings for Rosh Hashanah ring with a divine appropriateness for the Millennium. *L'Shana Tova*—for a good year, and *Tikatayou* —"may you be inscribed in the Book of Life for the coming year."

This ten day period of celebration ends with the Feast of Atonement (Yom Kippur) when God's judgment is sealed. Then comes the week-long celebration of the Feast of Tabernacles when man reflects on the fragile texture of life without God, and how dependent on Him we are for our existence. It is the time of harvest and the great ingathering of souls before and after the Second Coming of Messiah.

Tabernacles will be the feast of the Millennium when representatives from each nation will be required to come Jerusalem for worship, if they want rain for their land and the blessings of God on their people. Zechariah warned that, "whoso will not come up of all the families of the earth unto Jerusalem to worship the King, the Lord of hosts, even upon them shall be no rain" (Zechariah 14:17).

For those who have an argument against "forced worship," in the Millennium it will be a law. Once a year every nation will send ambassadors to Jerusalem. Secretaries of State, Presidents, Premiers, and Monarchs will turn their private planes toward Israel, and each will personally pay homage to the King.

Finally, as we conclude our look at the coming millennial celebrations, I want to call your attention to one more feast observed by Israel which the Apostle Paul referred to as "a shadow of things to come." It is called *Rosh Hodesh*, the "Feast of the New Moon."

For centuries, pagan religions have mistakenly worshiped the heavenly bodies and charted their lives by the rising of the New Moon. But God has an altogether different purpose for His people concerning the full lunar reflection. At the ancient celebration of *Rosh Hodesh*, all business transactions ceased, families came together with thank offerings, and special sacrifices were made by the priests. It was a time for gatherings, feasting, and worship. Basically, however, the New Moon celebration was God's way of calling His people to dedicate each new month to Him—to make Him a daily and a continual part of their lives, their work and their worship.

Through weekly Sabbaths, monthly New Moon dedications, the Feasts of Passover, Pentecost, and Tabernacles with their various offerings and dedications—ancient Israel was trained and educated for a life of worship, work, and celebration "heaven style." So will the millennial man be trained and educated. Then will Jesus' 2,000 year-old prayer finally be answered.

Yes, even the Son of God has prayers that are yet to receive an answer. "Thy kingdom come, thy will be done on earth as it is in heaven," will not be answered until the Millennium. Not until man learns to live in the awareness of God, to celebrate His presence within us and among us—not until we can welcome Him into all that we are and all that we do, will we be ready for the Father's arrival.

> Then comes the end, when He delivers the kingdom to God the Father, when He puts an end to all rule and all authority and power. For He [Jesus] must reign till He has put all enemies under His feet. The last enemy that will be destroyed is death. For 'He [God] has put all things under His [Jesus] feet.' But when He says 'all things are put under Him,'...then

the Son Himself will also be subject to Him who put
all things under Him, that God may be all in all. (1
Corinthians 15:24-28)

The Millennium is a period of 1,000 years during which
Jesus will come down to earth and prepare all living things
for the coming of the living God. It is a celebration that
finds its richest expression in worship.

The Restoration of Davidic Worship

Worship of God is fundamental to restoring life on
planet earth. Correct understanding of God is paramount.
God is not a religion of ideals and arbitrary standards. God
is the first cause, the eternal, self-existent Person from
whom all life issues. He alone is to be worshiped and
praised, and it is to be done in the manner of His choos-
ing.

Thus, when David was preparing to bring the Ark of
the covenant into Jerusalem, after he had set apart the
priests and purified them, he appointed musicians to accompany the ark. Three men were selected to be the chief
musicians as singers and players of instruments—along
with fourteen assistants. Three national choirs were established in Israel: The Levites (men), the Alamoth (women
singers and musicians), and men singers.

These three choirs with silver trumpets, cymbals, psal-
teries, and harps, a choir director and the King formed a
grand processional of music, leaping and dancing as the
ark moved toward Jerusalem. I believe this is a type of the
glorious procession that will accompany Jesus as He descends from heaven to make war with Satan's emissaries
at Armageddon. I do not believe the Church will be a sol-

emn assembly of intimidated spectators. The sounds of praise that will be accompanying us will be the "Shout of a King!" even as was reported of Israel when they came out of Egypt. Balaam said, "One shout of a King is among them!"

David's processional into the city of Jerusalem with the ark was a miniature of the greater heavenly processional that you and I will experience as we accompany our Lord at the end of this age.

> David was clothed with a robe of fine linen, as were all the Levites who bore the ark, the singers, and Chenaniah the music master with the singers. David also wore a linen ephod. Thus all Israel brought up the ark of the covenant of the Lord with shouting and with the sound of the horn, with trumpets and with cymbals, making music with stringed instruments and harps. (1 Chronicles 15:27,28)

After offering sacrifices to the Lord, David's choirs sang a song of thanksgiving composed by David wherein he admonished the people to make God's deeds known among the people. He praised God for His covenant with His people, he thanked Him for His works in nature, and finally he praised God for His eternal goodness and mercy to save His people. Following this three-day service, permanent musicians were appointed to minister in praises and thanksgivings to God.

According to John's revelation there will be various choirs singing at the coming of Jesus. In Revelation 5:9,10 we hear a chorus of the twenty-four elders singing: "And they sang a new song, saying: 'You are worthy to take the scroll, and to open its seals; for You were slain, and have redeemed us to God by Your blood out of every tribe and tongue and people and nation, and have made us kings and priests to our God; and we shall reign on the earth.'"

Do you know that an innumerable choir will sing the song of Moses? During the Millennium a magnificent choir of countless people will be singing these words,

> I will sing to the Lord, for He has triumphed gloriously! The horse and its rider He has thrown into the sea! The Lord is my strength and song, and He has become my salvation; He is my God, and I will praise Him; my father's God, and I will exalt Him. The Lord is a man of war; the Lord is His name. Pharaoh's chariots and his army He has cast into the sea; his chosen captains also are drowned in the Red Sea. The depths have covered them; they sank to the bottom like a stone. Your right hand, O Lord, has become glorious in power; Your right hand, O Lord, has dashed the enemy in pieces. And in the greatness of Your excellence You have overthrown those who rose against You; You sent forth Your wrath which consumed them like stubble. And with the blast of Your nostrils the waters were gathered together; the floods stood upright like a heap; and the depths congealed in the heart of the sea. The enemy said, "I will pursue, I will overtake, I will divide the spoil; my desire shall be satisfied on them. I will divide the spoil; my desire shall be satisfied on them. I will draw my sword, my hand shall destroy them."(Exodus 15:1-9)

A choir will also sing the song of the Lamb (Revelation 15:2). Revelation 14:3 tells about a choir of 144 thousand redeemed who will sing a song that only they know. It will be a special composition birthed by the Spirit just for them to sing.

All the People Will Sing

Have you ever wondered why Davidic-Hebraic music has returned to the church? Surely the first believers, who were Jewish, sang the Psalms. Why then, is that Hebraic fervor returning to worship music? We sing it in our services regularly, along with thousands of other congregations all over the world. I believe it is a definite signal of the millennial worship that is soon coming. Let us talk for a moment about Davidic worship. Davidic worship included "all the people." The king danced and played before the Lord, the priests, the musicians, the neighbors—each brought such worship as he was equipped to bring. Indeed, who will not worship when the King leads the way? Except those who sit looking out the window of self-serving ungodliness, as did Michal the wife of the king. There are always those who have no appreciation for sacred things and are offended by heartfelt expressions to God. They do not understand the motive of the worshiper. We worship God that all may be blessed of God. It is a hunger for the blessing of God so deeply embedded within the heart of the worshiper that drives him to risk becoming a spectacle in order to gain a greater measure of God. A worshiper is a warrior, a desperate, even violent man who will risk everything if need be, in order to be a part of the divine blessing.

Wherever the ark went that family or city was blessed. David wanted the blessing of God. So do we. Wherever Christ the Ark is received we are blessed. Each church service is a gathering before the Ark of God—music, singing, instruments, dancing and leaping are in order. Worship led by dedicated, clean, consecrated musicians will honor The Ark of Christ and bring down the blessing. All but the Michal-heart that does not know Him may be swept into the blessing.

Yet, those who hunger for the blessing of worship must be mindful of David's first failure to please God. God is not pleased unless He is honored. He is not honored unless He is obeyed. This means that obedience to the Word coupled with due reverence must frame the worship of God, if we will receive the blessing. Without overemphasizing temporal things, God's judgment on Uzzah for touching the ark, teaches those who would worship that those things which assist us in worship are to be respected. The sanctuary should be respected, Bibles, vessels for the Lord's Supper have been set apart for sacred use. A sense of reverence is appropriate in the house of God—not the traditional whisper, but an attitude of wholeheartedly seeking to honor God's presence, and hear His voice.

Only God knows the heart that is truly seeking Him— sometimes referred to as "the set of the soul." The volume of worship, either loud or soft, says nothing about the true "set of the soul." A soul is set even before it arrives in the service. A hungry person does not go to the restaurant in order that he may get hungry, his hunger is what drives him to the restaurant. Worship does not drive us to God, it is the doorway through which those who have set their face to reach Him may enter in. The "preparation" for worship is the lifestyle outside the church, and has direct bearing on what will occur during worship.

Essentially, worship is the one "right" thing man can do. The world is forever telling the Church to stop meeting in worship so often and get out and "give to the poor," "give to the hurting," "give to the hungry,"—and these are charitable, Christian deeds. But what we owe to ourselves and each other is never to eliminate our primary responsibility to "give unto the Lord the glory due his name."

First and foremost in every person's life is the responsibility to be a public worshiper of God.

Epilogue

A Glimpse of Eternity

There is going to be a wedding. Exactly how the ceremony will be performed is not clear, but a marriage between heaven and earth is certain.

In Revelation 19, John writes of the day of Jesus' arrival on earth that, "the marriage of the Lamb is come and his wife hath made herself ready...blessed are they which are called unto the marriage supper of the Lamb..." (Verses 7,9).

After describing the descent of Jesus from heaven, accompanied by an army of saints and angels, John records God's call to the birds of the air, saying to all the fowls that fly in the midst of heaven, "Come and gather yourselves together unto the Supper of the great God" (verse 17).

This puts the Marriage Supper of the Lamb at Armageddon in the land of Israel. It describes the menu as the armies of those who are there seeking to annihilate the statehood of Israel. But when these same armies see Jesus they turn to make war with Him. John writes: "And I saw the beast, the kings of the earth, and their armies, gathered together to make war against Him who sat on the horse and against His army" (Revelation 19:19).

Then John says of the armies that oppose Christ, "All the fowls were filled with their flesh" (verse 21). The location of the Marriage Supper is Israel. The menu is the godless armies of the nations who have joined the world class political genius called the Antichrist. The guests are the immortal saints, the angels, and the people of Israel.

The Bride Comes

In an effort to console His disciples about His impending death, Jesus once made the following statement:

> Let not your heart be troubled; you believe in God, believe also in Me. In My Father's house are many mansions; if it were not so, I would have told you. I go to prepare a place for you. And if I go and prepare a place for you, I will come again and receive you to Myself; that where I am, there you may be also. (John 14:1-3)

Traditionally, the Church has always assumed this to mean that Jesus would be going back to heaven to prepare a place for the believers. At death we would then go there to live with Him forever, and heaven would be our home. But may I suggest that what Jesus was actually saying was this: Jesus was going back to the heavenly Jerusalem where He would prepare a glorious residence for each believer. Those who died before Jesus' return to earth would immediately occupy their residence. But there would be a generation that would not die, and Jesus must also prepare a home for them in the eternal city.

When the city is completed and all residences are built, He will come in the clouds and gather together all believers both in heaven and on earth, and as one great com-pany we will descend back to earth for the end of human government and the celebration of the marriage feast. This marks the beginning of the Millennium. Then, for 1,000 years, the earth will undergo preparation to receive New Jerusalem—for the full consummation of the marriage, about which John wrote:

> Then I, John, saw the holy city, New Jerusalem, coming down out of heaven from God, prepared as a bride adorned for her husband. And I heard a loud voice from heaven saying, 'Behold, the tabernacle of God is with men, and He will dwell with them, and they shall be His people, and God Himself will be with them and be their God'.... Then one of the angels who had the seven bowls filled with the seven last plagues came to me and talked with me, saying, 'Come, I will show you the bride, the Lamb's wife.' And He carried me away in the Spirit to a great and high mountain, and showed me the great city, the holy Jerusalem, descending out of heaven from God, having the glory of God. And her light was like a most precious stone, like a jasper stone, clear as crystal. (Revelation 21:2,3,9-11)

The Bride is New Jerusalem—the city of God, the throne of God, and the immortal saints of God, of all ages. According to Hebrews eleven, it is the city that has been prepared for all believers, from faithful Abel to the martyrs of the New Testament Church and until the moment of the Rapture. The Bride is not only buildings, nor is it only people. The Bride of Christ includes the full wedding party. Without the throne of God, the Bride is not complete. Without the people of God, the city is not complete. We need to see the full spectrum of God's plan if we will catch a preview of the marriage that is to come. I suggest that the consummation of the marriage of Christ with His bride will take place 1,000 years after the wedding supper [which in God's sight is one day, 2 Peter 3:8]. It will be a union for eternity.

The beauty and architectural splendor of the eternal city of God is beyond description. John used pearls and precious gems and metals to describe its color and brilliance. But it will not only be a work of beauty to be admired. New Jerusalem is and will continue to be totally functional. John declared that, "...The nations of those who are saved shall walk in its light, and the kings of the earth bring their glory and honor into it. Its gates shall not be shut at all by day (there shall be no night there). And they shall bring the glory and the honor of the nations into it" (Revelation 21:24-26).

The universe is and will continue to be run from New Jerusalem. Whereas all nations will answer to earthly Jerusalem during the Millennium, in eternity all creation will answer to heavenly New Jerusalem.

A celestial phenomenon will one day occur in the heavens. At the end of the Millennium, a brilliant planet will begin to move from the outermost regions of creation toward the Milky Way. It will not be a comet that whizzes across the sky and then disappears into the darkness, but this planet will—as it were—move with pomp and majesty at a pace every eye can see. Accompanied by a heaven illuminated seven times brighter than we know today, this

New Jerusalem planet will glide as a bride down the aisles of space until it reaches the longing sphere of its Eternal Groom.

And waiting on planet earth to receive her will be the Son of God. Then forever, New Jerusalem with its saints, and the earth with its redeemed, will shine as two flawless, blue-white diamonds, bound together with Christ, in the mystery of the ages. It is the mystery of God's will which Paul says was God's "good pleasure which he purposed Himself, that in the dispensation of the fullness of times He might gather together in one all things in Christ, both which are in heaven and which are on the earth—in Him" (Ephesians 1:9,10).

THE COMPANION INDEX
FOR GROUP DISCUSSION OR
PERSONAL EVALUATION

Welcome to *The Companion Index*—the perfect answer to remembering what you have learned. Whether it be a book, a sermon, or a teaching, the value of our time is weighed by how much of the material we retain. Group discussion and/or personal testing is a proven method for helping people to clarify and remember what they have learned.

The Companion Index is a booklet designed for group study or personal evaluation. It opens with a series of general questions on the subject. It then takes each chapter—giving a brief summary of the material covered and follows with a series of stimulating questions designed to help you master the key points of the chapter.

If you are not already a teacher of others, you can be. "Make disciples" was our Lord's great and final commission. It is my sincere desire that your own personal growth from this book will enrich the lives of many. Nothing is more rewarding than helping people to grow in understanding of God.

MONA JOHNIAN

INTRODUCTION

<u>Life in the Millennium</u>

I have been speaking and writing on the subject of End Times for years. Until now a part of that subject called the Millennium has been largely unexplored. Now that I have discovered it in Scripture, I find evidence of the Millennium everywhere I turn in both Old and New Testaments. And what a discovery! From pulpit to pew, the Millennium is one of the most relevant subjects of this generation. It is in fact the next great program of God. With the book "Life in the Millennium" and the Companion Index, you can begin your own investigation into this enriching subject, as well as discover a greatness in God you never knew existed.

But before we begin our chapter by chapter question and answer discussion I thought you might like to see how many of the following questions you can answer.

SECTION I

Questions:

1. What is the Millennium?

2. Who will rule in the millennial kingdom age?

3. When will Christ begin His reign?

4. Where will His capital buildings be located?

5. How long will Christ rule from Israel?

6. Who will rule under Christ?

7. Isn't the kingdom of heaven already here? Jesus said the kingdom is within you.

8. Where can I find information on the millennial kingdom of Christ?

9. Will there be unbelievers during the Millennium?

10. What if someone violates the kingdom laws during the Millennium?

11. Are the Millennium and Eternity the same thing?

12. What is the purpose of the Millennium?

(Answers on the Next Page)

Answers:

1. The word millennium comes from the Latin "Mille Annus" and means 1,000 years. In Scripture Millennium means the coming kingdom age for 1,000 years.

2. Jesus Christ (Messiah) will be the Sovereign Authority throughout the Millennium. (Revelation 20:4,6).

3. The Millennium will begin when Jesus returns to earth (Revelation 11:15).

4. Jerusalem, Israel will be the capital of the earth, (Zechariah 14:17/Ezekiel 40-48).

5. The Millennium will last for one thousand years (Revelation 20:4,6).

6. Leadership under the Messiah include; David who will be resurrected to rule as prince over Israel (Jeremiah 30:4,89). The twelve apostles of Christ who will rule, one over each of the twelve tribes of Israel (Matthew 19:27,28). The Church that will rule in various administrative positions over the gentile nations (Revelation 5:10).

7. The Spirit of the kingdom is in the heart of each believer, but its replacement of human government over the face of the earth has yet to be fully implemented (Revelation 1:15).

8. The subject of the Millennium is throughout the Bible. It is clearly identified in David (Chronicles 17:11-

14). The most comprehensive address of the Millennium is the book of Isaiah. Revelation 20 specifically refers to the 1,000 years reign of Christ and His people four times.

9. Yes, there will be unbelievers in the Millennium. They will not be so active in their sin however. Satan will be bound, leaving them content to obey Christ's strict kingdom laws. (See Zechariah 14:17,18). Unbelievers will rebel at the end of the Millennium. (See Revelation 20).

10. Rebellion will be dealt with promptly, possibly with death (Isaiah 11:4).

11. No, the Millennium and Eternity are not the same. In eternity, the universal kingdom of God will be firmly established over all creation. The Millennium is a phase of the universal kingdom (1 Corinthians 15:24-28).

12. The purpose of the Millennium is for resolution and restoration. During the Millennium, Christ will resolve:
- The conflict over the land of Israel.
- The age old war between good and evil.
- Make all powers subject to God.
- Cleanse the earth of sin's pollution.
- Prepare the earth for eternity.

SECTION II

Now that you have answered these questions would you care to tackle some more weighty thoughts on the subject of man's eternal destiny?

This section covers each chapter 1-16 of the book, "Life in the Millennium" After you have mastered these topics for yourself, try them in a group discussion or with your friends. The Scriptures were written for all believers, including the subject of end time events and the New Age that is coming. You will be greatly enriched as you discuss and grow in understanding of the Millennium.

QUESTIONS & ANSWERS
FOR GROUP DISCUSSION
ON EACH CHAPTER OR PERSONAL STUDY

CHAPTER 1
The New World Order

"Eye has not seen, nor ear heard nor have entered into the heart of man the things which God has prepared for those who love Him." During the millennium, man will no longer be bound by the limitations of this fallen world. He will operate through a mind patterned after God's, with unlimited ability. Man and his world will be brought through a process of cleansing and the curse will be dismissed. God, the master surgeon, will remove Satan's headquarters as well as Satan himself and his influence over this earth. Our worn, torn planet will be revitalized and then will come the new world order.

1. Who will experience 1,000 years of unhindered growth and development?
   Answer: page 1.

2. Why are we, in this present age, not operating within the intellectual and creative realm of potential that God originally intended for us?
   Answer: page 2.

3. What did the sacrificial death of Jesus do for the earth and its inhabitants?
   Answer: page 3.

4. Exactly when and by whom will Satan's headquarters be eliminated?

Answer: page 5.

5. When Satan's headquarters are removed, what will become of the second heavens? (Provide a biblical reference which supports your answer.)

Answer: Consider Isaiah 30:26.

6. What is the overall purpose of the millennium and what will it serve to usher in?

Answer: pages 6,7.

7. How must worship be conducted and what does it accomplish in man?

Answer: pages 10,11.

8. What will be the very first thing restored by Jesus during His millennial reign and what effect will it have on man?

Answer: page 13.

9. What vital spiritual senses will be fully restored to man during the millennium and what biblical reference leads us to understand this truth?

Answer: pages 13,1,2.

CHAPTER 2
The Twilight of the Tribulation Passover

This chapter discusses God's original mandate to the nation Israel. Since Abraham had been chosen to establish the Messianic line from which the Savior of the world would come, it was necessary that his descendants possess the land where Messiah would be born. This land was Israel.

Abraham fathered Isaac, Isaac fathered Jacob. God changed Jacob's name to Israel and gave him twelve sons. When Jacob was near death, he called in his twelve sons and prophetically passed down their spiritual blessing. To his son Judah he gave the mandate to hold on to the land of Israel as a lion holds on to his prey. Jesus the Messiah would come from the tribe of Judah.

1. What did Jacob mean when he said, "The scepter shall not depart from Judah, nor a lawgiver from between his feet, until Shiloh comes; and to Him shall be the obedience of the people." (Genesis 49:10).
Answer: page 18.

2. The natural out working of the destiny of the human race was laid upon the shoulders of Israel. Can you list several examples of how God has used Israel to bring about the plan of salvation?
Answer: Page 19.

3. The nation Israel was driven out of their land in what year? What year did they return?
Answer: page 18.

4. The stage for the world theater of end time events is located where?

Answer: page 20.

5. The price for redemption (salvation) was legally ratified at Calvary. When will this plan be completely implemented on earth?

Answer: page 22.

6. What does Acts 3:21 mean?

Answer: page 21.

7. Although the nation Israel and the Church are under the same Commander, is their program the same?

Answer: page 22.

8. For discussion: Why is it important for the Church to recognize the nation Israel?

CHAPTERS 3-5
The Coming Exodus
The Great Contest
The Last Great Army

These three chapters discuss seven examples of Israel's experiences under persecution during their days of enslavement in Egypt. This should make interesting, even debatable material for group discussion.

1. Do the experiences of Israel apply to the Church?
   Answer: pages 23,24.

2. Will everything be restored immediately or gradually after Jesus returns?
   Answer: page 25.

3. Discuss the term "Church" does it apply only to Gentiles since the Crucifixion?
   Answer: pages 26,27.

4. There are seven examples listed that happened to Israel during their bondage in Egypt that may parallel end time events and the Church. Discuss briefly each example.
   Example #1 - pages 30,31
   Example #2 - pages 31-32
   Example #3 - pages 33-36
   Example #4 - pages 40-43
   Example #5 - pages 43-45
   Example #6 - pages 45-55
   Example #7 - pages 61-67

CHAPTERS 6-7
The Church Raptured
Israel Rescued

Chapter six and seven introduce one of the most controversial subjects of eschatology—the rapture of the Church. They cover the Seven seals seen by John in Revelation chapter 5 and leave room for various positions on the subject of the rapture. Also enclosed are the seven trumpets and seven vials of Revelation. The seven seals, seven trumpets and seven vials represent twenty-one events that will occur during the last seven years before the Coming of Jesus. They are events consisting basically of:

> wars
> cosmic disturbances
> weather changes
> pestilence
> disease
> demonic activity

1. What are the Seven Seals?
   Answer: pages 74-81; 88-90.

2. The trumpets are blown at the breaking of the Seventh Seal. List the events of the Seven Trumpets.
   Answer: pages 90-91.

3. The Seven Vials follow the Seven Trumpets. Discus the Seven Vials.
   Answer: pages 92-93.

CHAPTER 8
The Millennial Throne

With the Church raptured and returned to earth with Jesus, with Israel rescued from national annihilation, the Millennial Age begins. The throne of the Messiah is the theme and focus of this New Age. Everything in the Millennium will revolve around the Messiah and His government. In these chapters we go back to King David where God first introduced Messiah Jesus' throne in the house of David.

1. What does God's promise in 1 Chronicles 17:11-14 have to do with the Kingdom Age of the Messiah?
   Answer: pages 99-101.

2. Discuss the parallels between Jesus and King David.
   Answer: pages 102-106.

CHAPTER 9
Will Sin Exist in the Millennium?

This chapter addresses sin and prayer during the Millennium. Do you envision the Millennium as a period of social perfection?

1. Read pages 101-108. Discuss "Separation of Church and State" in the Millennium. Will it exist? If not, why not?

2. Read pages 108-113 and discuss the keys to effective praying.

CHAPTER 10
The Unbroken Good Work

This chapter addresses the work of God in a person's life and in the world as a whole.

1. Read pages 121-123 and discuss God's work in a world of changing circumstances.

2. What do you think about a "Second Pentecost?" (See pages 128-129).

Food For Thought:
     Does God ever change His plans because of natural circumstances? Do you believe there is an unconditional will or plan of God that cannot be altered—such as the birth of Christ and His Coming again? If so, do you also believe some of His plans are conditional based on man's actions? (Refer to 1 Samuel 13).

CHAPTER 11
Prosperity Is Coming

Chapter twelve is an encouraging look at the changes in nature that are coming during the Millennium.

1. Will the Antichrist prevail?
   Answer: page 133-134.

2. What is the ultimate purpose of all creation?
   Answer: page 135.

3. Do you believe the serpent literally conversed with Eve?
   Answer: page 136.

4. What major changes are coming into the wild animal kingdom during the Millennium, and what brings about these changes?
   Answer: pages 136-140.

CHAPTER 12
The Desert Will Bloom

1. Discuss the future significance of Iraq. Refer to pages 141-145.

2. Which do you consider more important to the Middle East—oil or water?
    Answer: pages 145-147.

3. Do you think sickness will disappear immediately or gradually upon the return of Christ to the earth?
    Answer: pages 150-152.

CHAPTER 13
An Ointment Poured Forth

1. Is there evidence of Christ in the Old Testament?
   Answer: page 155-157.

2. Do you envision God and Christ as two separate entities? (See Psalm 2:2,7). How much of Father God do you think the saints will see? Refer to pages 157-158.

3. Do you think the Church understands the use of the name of Jesus? How do you use His name?
   Answer: pages 158-162.

CHAPTER 14
Forty Days into the Future

This chapter explores what resurrection man will be like in the Millennium and eternity. Contrary to popular thinking, the distant heavens is not the final destiny of believers. Heaven is a mediatorial place where we go at death. At Jesus' second coming however, the dead bodies of those in Christ, along with all living believers will be raptured and return to earth with Christ to rule and reign for a thousand years.

There is a "divine continuity" that never allows the soul of man to lose touch with his physical body. Although death separates the soul from the body the two are permanently linked forever. Believers can expect to have their bodies returned in a glorified state at the coming of Jesus. The fact of resurrection has been since the creation of man. Scripture records at least nine people who returned from death. We have a promising future!

1. How was Elisha the prophet involved in a resurrection?

Answer: page 163.

2. Historically the world has always held one of two views concerning life after death. What are they?

Answer: page 165.

3. What will resurrected Man be like during the Millennium?

Answer: pages 169.

CHAPTER 15
Ruling and Reigning

This chapter discusses the rulers of the Millennium. Scripture is quite clear that Jesus and the Gentiles will be in their own distinct countries. The controversy over borders will cease during the Millennium.

1. Read Isaiah 2:2-4 (pp. 173-4). What do you think the statement means, "He shall judge between the nations, and shall rebuke many people...?

2. Will there be unbelievers during the millennium?
 Answer: page 75 (Zechariah 14:16-19).

3. Read pages 176-177. List the order and ruling position during the Millennium of the following:

> Jesus
> King David
> The Twelve Disciples
> The Church

4. Question. What is going to happen to the unbelievers at the end of the Millennium?
 Answer: pages 180-181.

CHAPTER 16
Celebrate!

A key characteristic of the Millennium will be the celebration of worship. In Ancient Israel God established three major feast days: Passover, Pentecost (Feast of Weeks), Feast of Tabernacles. He gave other feasts five of which are:

>   A weekly sabboth,
>   Unleavened bread,
>   First fruits,
>   Trumpets,
>   Atonement.

1. Is observing the Sabbath important today?
   Answer: pages 185-187.

2. What is the significance of the Feast of Passover?
   Answer: page 188-89.

3. What is the significance of the Feast of Pentecost?
   Answer: page 189.

4. What is the Feast of Tabernacles?
   Answer: page 190.

5. The Feast of Firsttfruits is associated with "Passover." It marked a time when the farmers went into the fields to set aside the firstfruits of their harvest for an offering. What do you consider some of the purposes of giving?

6. How does the Christian relate to the Feast of Atonement?

Answer: page 190.

7. For discussion: What do you consider the primary purpose of worship to be?

8. For discussion: The Jews, both ancient and modern move their bodies back and forth as they pray, in response to God's command to seek Him with all "your might." What do you consider appropriate physical involvement in prayer?

9. Question: The Jews, both ancient and modern, dance around the Word of God on specific occasion. David and a host of people danced before the ark as it came into Jerusalem. How much physical involvement should the body have in worship today? (Refer to pages 169-170.)

10. For discussion: The Gnostics considered the body totally unholy. They believed Jesus to be a little less than God, as the Holy God would never submit to entering an unholy body. How do you view the body?

11. Question: What is the balance between body worship and body hatred prevalent today? How do we account for such popular trends as:
  • sensuous advertising
  • excessive dieting
  • dietary hang-ups (anorexia and bulimia)

- vegetarianism
- pagan flagellation
- sexual abuse and perversions
- physical abuse?

12. For discussion: What about proper burial of the body. How do you view cremation?

Speaking Engagements
and
Teaching Seminars

Mona Johnian is available for seminars or other speaking engagements throughout the year for churches, conferences, and colleges.

Subjects included are:

- "God's Message to the Nations"
- "Countdown to the Millennium"
- "Heaven"
- "Life in the Millennium"
- "Life in Eternity"
- "The Great Awards Day"
- "The Marriage Supper"
- "The Coming Antichrist"

Please Contact:

Mona Johnian
Christian Teaching and Worship Center
P.O. Box 391
Winchester, MA 01890
(617) 935-5117